THE BEGGARS

STRIKE

THE BEGGARS' STRIKE

STRIKE

OR THE DREGS OF SOCIETY

Aminata Sow Fall

translated by
Dorothy S. Blair

Longman

Longman Group UK Limited
Longman House, Burnt Mill,
Harlow, Essex

First published 1979 in Dakar by Les Nouvelles Editions
Africaines as *La Grève des Bàttu*
First published in Longman Drumbeat 1981
First published in Longman African Classics 1986

Produced by Longman Group (FE) Ltd
Printed in Hong Kong

ISBN 0-582-00243-5

By way of a glossary

In this English version of Aminata Sow Fall's novel, I have kept some local terms which add to the 'local colour' or for which there is no good English equivalent. Some of these words are current in French-speaking West Africa, like *Toubab* used to designate a Frenchman or woman; others are from Wolof, the language spoken by the majority of Senegalese.

The beggars, about whom this story is told, are referred to by the author as *boroom bàttu*, literally, 'holders of calabashes' or begging-bowl-bearers, as the *bàttu* which they hold out for alms is a little calabash.

Certain words refer specifically to aspects of an Islamic society:

MARABOUT a saintly Muslim teacher or holy man, sometimes a hermit and usually distinguished by his asceticism. Marabouts are widely consulted for advice on many material and practical problems of existence and in contemporary Senegalese works of fiction there is a tendency to criticise the hold they have over the population.

SERIGNE a leader of Islamic community, thence a title of respect used when addressing a marabout.

TALIBÉ the disciple of a marabout. Mainly used to apply to children who are handed over while very young to the care of a marabout from whom they receive instruction in the Koran. They live with the marabout and have to go out each day to beg for their own and their master's subsistence.

TISBAAR one of the five obligatory daily prayers; to be said at noon.

The following words refer to articles of clothing worn in Senegal:

BOUBOU a long and usually voluminous outer garment, worn by both men and women; a sort of caftan.

PAGNE a simpler garment, of varying length, worn

under the boubou, sometimes draped around the waist, but incorrectly translated by 'loin-cloth'. Literally, a length of cloth.

BEECO a little pagne, worn under a larger and longer pagne. This would more closely correspond to a 'loin-cloth'.

TURKI like a pagne, a garment worn under the boubou.

CHÉCHIA a silk or cotton scarf draped around the head and neck.

The following are culinary terms referring to food or drink:

COUSCOUS a dish made of ground millet, served with fish or meat and various tasty sauces.

BAASI SALTE a local dish, as prepared in Cayor and as prepared in Jolof; i.e. two kingdoms which played an important role in the pre-colonial history of Senegal.

KINKILEBA a refreshing infusion made from the dried leaves of a local bush.

The author offers the following explanation and etymology for the name 'Kifi Bokoul' that she gives to the mystic marabout introduced in chapter 8 and the fictional 'legend' she tells about his birth:

Ki = the one; fi = here; Bokoul = does not belong; so Kifi Bokoul is 'the one who does not belong here' or 'is not of this earth'.

A *kora* is a musical instrument with between sixteen and thirty-two strings, akin to a European harp.

D. S. BLAIR

Hark! Hark! no dogs do bark!
No beggars are coming to town ...
(With apologies to the English nursery
rhyme. Translator)

Chapter One

This morning there has been another article about it in the newspaper: about how the streets are congested with these beggars, these *talibés*, these lepers and cripples, all these derelicts. The Capital must be cleared of these people – parodies of human beings rather – these dregs of society who beset you everywhere and attack you without provocation at all times. You hope that the traffic-lights will never turn red as you approach an intersection in your car! And once you've overcome the obstacle of the traffic-lights, you have to get past another hurdle to reach the hospital, force your way through a bombardment to get to work in your own office, struggle to emerge from the bank, make a thousand detours to avoid them at the markets, and finally pay a ransom to enter the House of God! Oh! these men, these parodies of human beings, as persistent as they are ubiquitous! The Capital is crying out to be cleared of them. If Keba Dabo had had any doubts about this before, he is now quite convinced, as once again he has found himself in a completely inadmissable situation. On Friday he had the misfortune to be in a Lebanese merchant's shop. Now, everyone knows that on Fridays the streets are clogged up with beggars. Just as a young man was coming out of the shop, a beggar was feeling his way in and hit him with his stick. The young man swore at the beggar; the latter came back at him with some choice obscenities, to everyone's stupefaction.

'How dare you use such language to me?'

'Oh! just because we're beggars, people think we're dogs! We're beginning to get fed up with the way we're treated!'

This just beats everyone. And it certainly beats Keba Dabo, when it is in fact his job to free the streets of this conglomeration of humanity. Keba Dabo is Assistant to Mour Ndiaye, the Director of the Department of Public Health and Hygiene. Mour Ndiaye had been absolutely categorical when he called his assistant into his office last week. In his right hand he held the memorandum from the Minister reiterating the order for the public highways to be cleaned up; with his left hand he motioned to Keba to take a seat in front of him.

'Keba, the situation is getting more and more worrying. These beggars, they ... well, they're making life a bit difficult for us, really. Didn't I tell you to do something about them?'

'Yes, sir. I carried out your instructions. I must say I can't understand it myself ... I don't know how they manage to get back on the streets. We organise raids every week; sometimes they're dropped more than a hundred miles away, but the next day they're back at their strategic points. It's really getting quite beyond me, sir.'

Keba did not tell Mour Ndiaye his feelings every time a beggar held out his hand to him. He did not tell him how he nearly choked when filthy hands were poked right into his car, as soon as he was imprudent enough to lower the windows, nor the remorse he felt when he conformed to the principle he had laid down never to give alms to beggars, a principle that was not inspired by meanness or churlishness, but simply because he was shocked to see human beings – however poor they might be – diminishing their own dignity by sponging on others in such a disgraceful, shameless fashion. He forgot that hunger and poverty compelled some of them to beg, and so remind those who were better off that paupers too existed.

'Keba, it's not a question of understanding, it's a question of finding some way of getting rid of these people. Our Department's reputation is at stake. Must we let ourselves be thought ineffectual, incompetent?'

Keba's eyes rested on the large silver signet ring, on which were engraved some cabalistic signs, and which adorned the fourth finger of Mour Ndiaye's left hand.

'You realise,' the latter went on, 'their presence is harmful to the prestige of our country; they are a running sore which should be kept hidden, at any rate in the Capital. This year the number of tourists has fallen considerably, in comparison with last year's figures, and it's almost certain that these beggars are to some extent responsible. We really can't let them invade our cities and form a threat to public hygiene and the national economy.'

'Right sir, we'll set up an effective plan of campaign. You can rely on me.'

Mour Ndiaye knew he could count on Keba. In the six years that the latter had worked under him, he had had the opportunity of appreciating his good qualities: conscientious, honest, a veritable glutton for work, in six years Keba had never taken a day off without good reason, never asked to borrow a single penny on the pretext that he couldn't make ends meet in these difficult times or that he couldn't see his way through to the end of the month. For all these reasons Mour thought highly of Keba, who was in fact the brains of the service. Mour had been appointed to this post for political reasons, a form of recognition from the government for his past unconditional activity as a militant in the Party. He was well aware of this, but nevertheless made it a point of honour to deserve the reward he had received; so he shifted all responsibility on to Keba, whom he knew to be competent; the main thing for him was that things should be done properly, so that he could get the credit for them. He was only interested in more titles, more honours, and for this end he systematically made use of Keba's capacities, being a methodical man with a clear idea of his goal. And besides, who knows if this business of the beggars successfully handled, might not be a good opportunity for promotion?

The track which leads to Keur Gallo, a village hidden in the depths of the bush, is rough and tortuous, but Kouli knows all the unexpected twists and turns. He shows not the slightest anxiety, not the smallest sign of nerves, in spite of the violent sandstorm which covers the windscreen of the Mercedes with a veil of ochre dust. One of Kouli's jobs is to drive his employer's wife once a month to Keur Gallo. Lolli, a devoted spouse, concerned

3

about her husband's future, goes there to consult Serigne Birama. Mour Ndiaye knows many marabouts, but in his eyes none can compare with Serigne Birama, the man whose disinterest, knowledge and wisdom have earned him Mour Ndiaye's unfailing respect, his immeasurable gratitude.

The population of Keur Gallo scarcely exceeds fifty souls. Anything which breaks the silence and monotony of existence is a great event there. So everyone who has not gone off to the fields rushes up at the sound of the car. The children who, a few minutes before, were performing a Koranic symphony around Serigne Birama, drop their tablets at the foot of the majestic baobab tree, which is the umbilicus of the whole village.

Lolli is already seated on one of the chairs which furnish Serigne Birama's hut when the latter arrives.

'Sokhna Lolli, Badiane, Badiane. How are the people of the City?'

'Sidibe, Sidibe, everyone is at peace, Sidibe.'

Kouli gets two lads to help him carry the bag of rice, the box of dried milk, the bars of soap, the sugar and tea which Mour Ndiaye presents regularly to Serigne Birama at the end of every month.

'*Jerejef.* Thank you. God who perceives your actions will reward you. And Mour? How is he?'

'He is very well, thanks be to God. He is much taken up with his work. They have really no time at all in his Department. He asks me to let you know that even if he does not come, he nevertheless thinks of you all the time. Do not forget him in your prayers.'

Serigne Birama is clearly pleased. Pleased with all the gifts from Mour Ndiaye, pleased also with the loyalty of a *talibé*, who has not forgotten him now that he has made good.

'How could I forget him in my prayers, when he always thinks of me? The word I spoke yesterday is still my word today. This is my message to him: let him have no fear; *Insh' Allah*, he can only go forward. He is made to be a leader, it is written in his star. *Insh' Allah*, he will be one of the small number of men who hold the destiny of the

4

country in their hands. Here, take hold of one of the beads of this rosary.'

Serigne Birama takes the bead from Lolli's two fingers, spatters it with his saliva, mutters inaudible words, telling the beads of the rosary over and over again as he does so. Finally, with a confident air, he places the rosary down on the sheepskin which does office as a prayer-rug and says to Lolli, 'It is quite clear; what I see is very clear. A star which shines, which shines ... Prosperity, happiness. Mour could have a very great surprise. Tell him to sacrifice a ram. All will be well, *Insh' Allah*.'

'We owe everything to you, Serigne. Rest assured that our good fortune will be yours too.'

In pronouncing these words before taking her leave of Serigne Birama, Lolli is simply echoing what Mour Ndiaye was in the habit of saying: 'I owe my present position to Serigne Birama. That man is remarkable. I was nothing, nothing at all when I got to know him. I owe him everything, I shall never be able to repay him.'

'Nothing at all.' Mour often thought of those difficult years when he had been given the sack from his job as clerk in the Civil Service, for having had words with his boss. He could not stand the bullying and the occasional gross insults he received from this European who, because he was aware of living in a conquered country, treated the inhabitants worse than dogs. 'No sir! I'd rather die than let a little twerp like this walk all over me! I'll bet he doesn't rate two beans in his own country. So he gets his own back on us blacks, to give himself the idea he's Mr Big. No, sir! I'm not having any. I'll show him I'm a man!'

And one day, Mour had answered back, he'd told his boss what he could do with his insults, and when his boss had simply sneered at him and when his fellow-blacks had sniggered – what sort of brothers did they think they were? – he had seen red and before he knew what he was doing he had raised his arm and inflicted a stinging blow on his poor boss's pink cheek.

Two weeks in prison. Years of unemployment. Sent to Coventry by his own family. A long period of lean kine, during which he spent his time lying around in the shade of the mango trees, or chasing the sun when the season turned cold.

And now all that is nothing but a memory, or rather, no longer counts for anything. His real memory is of the day he met Serigne Birama, that distant day of sultry heat. Serigne Birama had come to the City to obtain an identity card, for the law obliged all citizens to possess one from that time. Not knowing how to read or write in the official language, he was unable to find his way about the maze of streets of the Capital. Overcome by thirst and exhaustion, he was quite lost on his way to the police station, where he had only been once in his life, when, like all the inhabitants of his village, he had gone to give moral support to one of his cousins who lived in the city, and who had got involved in a matter of receiving stolen property. Chance had guided his steps to the courtyard of a house and to the foot of a mango tree where Mour was enjoying the benefit of the shade. After the customary exchange of greetings, the latter had, at the request of this unknown visitor to the city, immediately hurried over to a container which stood in a corner at the other end of the courtyard and come back with a pitcher full of water. Nothing very elegant in this rusty tin-can that had once held canned tomatoes, now converted into a makeshift water-jug with a jagged rim. Such matters held no importance for Serigne Birama. As he put his parched lips to the refreshing liquid, he felt the ineffable sweetness of existence flow once more through his veins. He thanked Mour Ndiaye from the bottom of his heart, and then Mour Ndiaye accompanied him to the police station, to stretch his legs a bit and to exchange a few friendly words with a companion who did not make him feel ashamed of being out of work.

'What is your name?'

'Mour Ndiaye.'

Mour studied Serigne Birama as the latter walked beside him with his eyes on the ground: tall, spare, light-skinned, wearing a straw hat and a white, loose-sleeved caftan, under which an indigo-dyed *turki* could be

6

glimpsed. From him there emanated an air of purity, of sanctity even, which made him seem older than his thirty years, for this is not normally perceived in men before they have unrolled a long reel of existence devoted to prayer and charitable deeds. Such men, with the inner strength that derives from their moral plenitude, seem to belong to another world. This air of gravity inspired awe rather than fear; the gaze in those sharp little eyes was almost hypnotic; those close-cut finger-nails at the end of the bony hands had taken on the appearance of a delicate whitish film from having been kept from the slightest contact with any impurity; in a word, the whole of this man's being aroused in Mour's mind a host of questions that he suppressed only out of decency and discretion. Where could this man have come from? Who was he? What is he thinking about? ...

'It's extraordinary, the City ... You spend your time running. Your life is spent going from one complication to another.'

'That is certain,' replied Mour Ndiaye. 'Things get more and more difficult.'

'Everybody's running, running. People have no time to stop a moment and help villagers find their way about. *Chei yalla!* Goodness me! Next to God, you have given me most valuable assistance. I would have died of thirst ... May God who knows what you most desire grant you all your wishes. You will come to Keur Gallo one day if you are able. The first man you ask where Serigne Birama Sidibe lives will bring you right to my house.'

Since that day twenty years have passed. Never has Mour had reason to doubt Serigne Birama Sidibe.

Chapter Two

All the beggars in the City have gathered in Salla Niang's courtyard for the daily draw on their subscription scheme: everyone puts down a premium of one hundred francs and the total sum thus collected – five thousand francs – is paid out to one or other of the subscribers; they are allowed to double or triple their stake and so increase their chances of 'winning' by as many times. Salla Niang collects the subscriptions, acting as banker and making no compromises or concessions. She's a woman with plenty of guts and knows how to call to order any recalcitrants who claim their takings from the day's begging are less than the one hundred francs needed to put down.

'It hurts you to have to fork out the dough, eh! And when you get the chance of pocketing it, *Bissimilai!* Then you're happy enough. You just listen: don't try your tricks on me, you hear! Out with the dough! Nobody's allowed tick. You can't tell me! Even on the worst days anyone can collect more than a hundred francs.'

'Not at every corner!' someone in the crowd ventures.

'You'd better learn to speak the truth! Name me any part of the City where it isn't everyone's first action, first thing in the morning, to give something to the beggars. Even in the white areas; the black *Toubabs* and the white *Toubabs* all respect this ritual. And if you're talking about the poor districts, then you've come to the wrong shop with that story; everyone knows the poor give more readily than the rich. So hand over the lolly, you bunch of skinflints!'

There is universal laughter as Salla Niang, from her chair in the doorway of her room, harangues the impressive crowd of beggars who fill the courtyard, carrying their *bàttu* – the calabash which serves as a begging-bowl. Salla Niang holds a winnowing-basket on her lap and as she speaks she counts the money in the basket. The crowd comprises men and women of all ages and sizes, some crippled, some hale and hearty, all depending on their outstretched hands for their daily pittance.

Among them is blind Ngirane Sarr, always correctly dressed with his tie, soiled starched collar, dark, gold-rimmed spectacles, invariable navy-blue suit and white stick. Nguirane Sarr has a somewhat distinguished air, perhaps because he always holds his head high and bent slightly to the left. His vantage point is the roundabout near the Presidential Palace where he regularly receives a coin, to which is associated a wish, from everyone who is about to obtain an audience with the President of the Republic. Charity opens doors, so here goes a final coin to open the door of the President's heart.

And among the faces like masks with darkly protruding eyes, among the hoary heads and ulcerated limbs, covered with the pustules of scabies or eaten away with leprosy, among the rags which leave half-naked bodies which have long been innocent of any contact with water, among the beggars' crutches, sticks and *bàttu*, there are some adorable little tots who smile happily at life, twittering in rhythm with the clatter of pewter jugs.

Here, among the teeming crowd, is Papa Gorgui Diop – the old man who has the knack of winkling an extra mite out of the donors, thanks to his extraordinary comic talent; he's a perfect scream, the way he acts an old man in love with a young girl; he portrays one by one each of the old man's three wives who make bawdy fun of their husband's fads, then the old man himself, trying to make himself out a youngster, and finally the mischievous young girl who first bleeds her elderly lover white and then gives him a kick in the backside. Gorgui Diop is well-known all over the City and people come a great distance to see him do his act in his accustomed pitch, in front of 'his' bank, from the twenty-fifth of the month to the tenth of the following month, and then at 'his' market from the eleventh onwards.

When the draw is over the beggars proceed to the sale of produce: rice, sugar, millet, biscuits, candles, sometimes a few chickens. The sole purchaser is Salla Niang who pays thirty per cent less than the normal price

9

for these goods, which serve to stock up the shop next to the house, which is managed by her husband. She's a real business woman is this Salla Niang. She had been in service as a maid-of-all-work, but had taken up begging as a career the day she gave birth to twins. One of her employers helped her to obtain a small plot of land, already cleared, on which she was able to build a house thanks to the proceeds from her begging. The twins are quite big now, so she can spend her days simply sitting in front of 'her' hospital, not too much in evidence, and send the children chasing after patients and visitors, while she keeps a strict watch out in case any competitors try to take advantage of their superior age and shamelessly do the children out of their takings.

It is newcomers who most often indulge in this unfair play, for the regulars respect the law of the underworld, and even if competition is hard with hands jostling each other under the noses of the donors who then throw a few coins at random, just to get rid of the beggars, even then they only take what actually falls into their own outstretched palms.

On the day we are talking about, there is only one absentee from Salla Niang's courtyard: that is Madiabel, the lame beggar. He had been a tinker in his native village, mending pots and pans. But fewer and fewer people brought cooking-pots with holes needing to be patched up or old saucepans needing new handles to be fixed. He couldn't sell any more cookers, for the agent who collected them and took them to the City to dispose of them had disappeared one fine day without paying him for the results of a whole year's work. Madiabel had two wives and eight children to feed and clothe, so one day he upped and left for the City and became a '*bàttu*-bearer' – without a *bàttu* – simply holding out his hand for alms. Business was much better and he was able regularly to send his family clothes and money for food.

On this particular day Salla Niang pointed out his absence as soon as the meeting started.

'Something's happened. Do you know what's the matter?'

'What's happened?'

'What's the matter?'

'It's not anything serious, is it?'

'Madiabel's had an accident,' Salla replied.

'*Ashunalla! Chei waai!* Oh dear! Oh dear! How dreadful!'

'How did it happen?'

'Where was the accident?'

'Is he dead?'

'Oh dear! Oh dear!'

'I don't know if he's dead or not,' said Salla. 'It seems the manager of "his" hotel complained to the police. They're bastards, those hotel people are. The police proceeded to organise a round-up. As he was trying to get away he ran out into the road without looking where he was going, just as a car came past at full speed.'

'Oh! those round-ups! They make our life a misery. Poor Madiabel! He shouldn't have run, with his lame leg. It must be fate.'

'Who wouldn't run, if he'd ever felt the sting of those whips? I take to my heels, I do, as soon as I catch sight of the fuzz. They lay about them like madmen; when they get worked up like that, they seem to forget that we're human beings.'

'Some of them are quite decent sorts,' Salla Niang intervenes. 'They've never picked me up in their round-ups; they've never laid a hand on me. As soon as I see them coming, I arrange my scarf neatly on my head, I settle myself comfortably on my bench and I tell the children not to be afraid and not to run.'

'The thing is, they don't take you for a beggar. In your smart *boubous* that are always freshly laundered and ironed, and with your children dressed as if they were going to a party, how could anyone imagine that you beg for a living?'

Everyone bursts out laughing. Poor Madiabel is forgotten. Narou, Salla's husband, happens to be passing at this moment with his kettle to go to his ablutions. He is delighted to hear the compliments addressed to his wife. Salla's *boubous* are very fine and she knows how to wear them. What is more, under her *boubou* she wears a *pagne*,

11

and under this pagne she wears an immaculate little loin-cloth, and under this she has strings of white beads round her hips. Women nowadays disdain this custom, not realising how much of their sexual attraction they lose thereby. The tinkle of these beads in the silence of the night in the Savanna, combined with the intoxicating smoke of *cuuraye* incense and the captivating perfume of *gongo* – what words can express the exhilarating effect this has on Narou!

'The old gossips in the district', he says to himself, 'will never understand that.'

'Narou is a weakling,' they say.

'Salla wears the trousers.'

'He's not really a man.'

'They can go on slandering me; not one of them will ever know what ties me to Salla.'

Chapter Three

'Here, marked in red, are their main vantage points. This time we must keep at it, make no concessions, keep on rounding them up. There must be daily rounds, from now on, instead of weekly. Yes, daily! We've got all the necessary means at our disposal: staff, cars, petrol. These folk have got to be cleared off all the streets in the Capital.'

Keba Dabo is holding a meeting of some twenty people in his office on the eighth floor of one of the administrative buildings – comfortable armchairs, marble floors, not a single fly to be seen. Keba Dabo addresses the men, and the men hold their notepads and pens and carefully follow the itinerary that Keba traces with a ruler on a map fixed to one of the walls, next to oriental hangings and pictures by famous artists.

'You must keep on the move throughout the City, until it's completely cleaned up. The Chief insists on this. He's received very clear instructions from the Minister.'

'Yes, Monsieur Dabo, but you know how it is … It's really very difficult.'

'This time, it's different; you've got to track them down wherever they lurk. They think they can wear us down, but if we have to take severe measures, we shall take severe measures. It's a very serious problem, you know. No one can move about freely any more, without being attacked wherever one goes. Now this is how we are going to proceed in future: we keep a systematic record of the identity of all the ones who are picked up – naturally we shall have to have a card-index. If it's their first offence, we shall try to reason with them, show them how degrading it is to exhibit themselves in the street, exposing their infirmities for profit. We must make them realise that begging lowers their dignity.'

'But Monsieur Dabo, it would be a complete waste of time. They won't even listen to us. They'll think we've gone out of our minds in fact!'

'Let's try, just the same. Persistent offenders will be given a good lesson and put on a truck for Mbada; that's two hundred miles away, a village where there's practically no means of transport, so how will they manage to get back here?'

'They'll still find some way of getting back!'

'If they come back they'll be put in prison! Yes, indeed! They'll land up in prison.'

'Well, that's a problem, too,' another of the men comments. 'The prison governors are complaining; they say the prisons are full up and these folk cost a lot to keep.'

'Listen, gentlemen! I think we're wasting our time in futile discussions. I'm convinced that daily round-ups, appeals to reason and dignity and a good lesson taught them in Mbada will succeed in getting rid of them. These people aren't animals after all; they're human beings, whatever you may think!'

Keba Dabo is optimistic. Every time the thought of a possible failure crosses his mind, he drives it away with a vigorous shake of his head. These people must be got rid of. It has become an obsession with him. He has an almost morbid fear of driving through the City, he's constantly afraid of meeting one and he has this choking sensation in his throat if one should unfortunately cross his path. His secretary, Sagar Diouf, an extremely nice-looking girl with whom he is on rather familiar terms, has told him not to get so worked up simply because there are some beggars about. She's sick of hearing him talking all the time about 'these folk who poison the air with their smell'. This has become his sole subject of conversation. And all these letters she has to type till her fingers are quite numb, and all these memos sent off to arrange meetings, all these messages to everyone, all because of a few beggars! It's quite beyond all reason.

And today again, when Keba Dabo has seen off the organisers of the various work-parties, he stops at the door of his secretary's office and tells her, beaming with pleasure, 'This time we'll get them. We'll succeed this time!'

Sagar replies, 'You know, Keba, you're wasting your

14

time with the beggars. They've been here since the time of our great-great-grandparents. They were there when you came into the world and they'll be there when you leave it. You can't do anything about them. In any case what's the idea of trying to get rid of them? What harm have they done you?'

'You don't understand, Sagar ... Don't you feel anything when they approach you ... no, it's not a matter of approaching – they accost you, they attack you, they jump out at you! That's it, they jump out at you! Don't you feel anything when they jump out at you?'

Sagar smiles, smoothes her frizzy black hair with her two hands and straightens her low-cut blouse.

'What do you think I should feel? If I've got anything to give them, I give it to them; otherwise I go on my way. That's all. And besides, religion teaches us we must help the poor. How could they live otherwise?'

'Religion prescribes help for the poor, but it doesn't tell the poor to cause continual disturbance to their neighbours. D'you hear, do you understand what I'm saying? It's you and your sort who encourage this plague. Has our religion ever blessed the man who loses all sense of shame?'

Sagar bursts out laughing and claps her hands together repeatedly. It's really too funny. She can't imagine how anyone can get so worked up about a stupid business of some beggars. She finds Keba more and more absurd.

'But tell me, Keba, just answer one question: how would they live if they didn't beg? And tell me this as well: who would people give alms to, as they have to give alms to someone, religion tells us so?'

Keba does not answer; he doesn't like having to find answers to questions like this; he prefers to evade them, as his business is to clean up the highways, to carry out his chief's orders and to get over this nausea that he feels at the sight of the beggars.

He goes back to his office, loosens his tie and flops down into an armchair. He feels as if he's suffocating. The vein on his forehead that runs back into his bushy hair now stands out prominently. Sagar Diouf has upset him again, but he restrains himself from getting wild with her. 'Sagar's not a bad kid; on the contrary ... But she's got no idea of really serious problems ... just like my wife. Women are more interested in frivolous things ... They've got to be taught responsibility ... It's only a question of education ... Fine clothes, pomp and ceremony, futile nonsense ... No, things can't go on like this ... But, on the other hand, some men don't like intelligent women, so they say; they're a threat to their superiority. Women who don't ask questions and who don't present any problems – that's what these cocksure fellows need, women they can treat like dolls ... Sagar looks like a doll with her dimpled cheeks. She's pretty as a doll. I don't know what could have caused her husband to have dished her ...'

The telephone rings.

'Hallo, yes. Hallo, Monsieur Ndiaye ... Good morning, sir. Yes, fine, thanks ... I'm pleased you've noticed it yourself. It'll soon be the same everywhere in the City. Very soon we shan't see any at all. Thank you, sir. Goodbye, sir.'

Mour Ndiaye is delighted. He realises all the advantages the success of this operation will mean to him. He has driven round the administrative district, glanced at every street corner, along every pavement, in front of the public buildings, and he didn't see a single beggar. 'Keba's a marvel. There's no one like him.'

A few days later he decides to go and visit Serigne Birama. He finds him sitting as usual in the shade of the majestic baobab tree, reading the Holy Book. Mour Ndiaye gives him a lift back in his car, to save him having to walk the two hundred yards or so to his house. In the boot of the car are the twenty pounds of sugar, the bag of rice, the carton of dried milk, the tea, cola-nuts and the packets of candles.

One of Serigne Birama's wives is sitting in the large courtyard of the house, surrounded by huge calabashes of ground millet and making the couscous. Mour Ndiaye greets her most cordially and throws her a thousand franc note. She immediately stands up and thanks him profusely, expressing endless wishes for his prosperity. Mour and Serigne Birama then go into one of the huts, the one where Serigne Birama receives his clients.

'Serigne, are you in good health?'

'*Maangi sant*, I thank the Creator. And many thanks to you too; *Jerejef*, after the Lord, I thank you. May He, who alone knows what you desire, fulfil your wishes.'

'Amen, amen, Sidibe! And are you still taking care of my little matters?'

'Have no fears on this score. All you have to do is to continue to say "Amen". If the prayers I say for you were drops of rain you would have drowned long ago. Mour, you can give thanks to the good Lord.'

'Yes, yes. I do give thanks to the good Lord, and I am most grateful to you. My tongue cannot express the feelings I have for you. I rely on you utterly. That is why I am going to speak to you of a most important matter. I have always told you all my difficulties. Lately I have had a lot of trouble with the beggars; in fact, that is the reason I have not been here for quite a long time.'

'You, having trouble with the beggars, you who gives so freely? Why should you have trouble with the beggars?'

'No, that's to say, it isn't me exactly ... It's the City authorities who are worrying about them. The beggars are an obstacle to the hygiene of the City ...'

'Dear me! The City is dehumanising you, hardening people's hearts so that they no longer pity the weak. Take care, Mour; God has said: "Let the poor come unto me".'

'Serigne, that's not the question. How can I explain ... Well, you see, nowadays, people who live a long way away, in Europe and the United States of America, White people especially, are beginning to take an interest in the beauty of our country. These people are called tourists. You know, in the old days these White people came to rob and exploit us; now they visit our country for a rest and in search of happiness. That is why we have built hotels and holiday villages and casinos to welcome them. These tourists spend huge sums of money to come here, there are even special societies over in Europe who organise

17

these journeys. And when these tourists visit the City, they are accosted by the beggars and we run the risk of their never coming back here or putting out unfavourable propaganda to discourage others who might like to come.'

'Dear me! I don't understand this. You City folk, you're the ones who understand these problems. So, nobody must beg there any more?'

'Serigne, times have changed. We are the ones now who are responsible for the destiny of our country. We must oppose anything which harms our economic and tourist development.'

Mour senses that Serigne Birama is displeased and he knows that his long argument has not convinced him.

'Serigne, what we really want, in the long run, is for everyone to get down to a proper job. We want to discourage idleness, so we exhort everyone to get down to work.'

'It is every man's duty to work.'

Mour has possibly forgotten the infirm and the elderly who haven't enough to eat. At all events, this is not important as far as he's concerned.

'Exactly! It's every man's duty to work. It's to make them work that we are driving them out of the City streets. It's a very difficult undertaking, this fight against an evil that has gained such a strong hold. We've been at it for years and now, thank God, I think we've got the upper hand. My Minister telephoned me to pass on the President's congratulations ... It isn't easy to get the President's congratulations; he's very difficult to please! That's why, when he deigns to congratulate anyone, it means he's really satisfied.'

'The President's congratulations will not rest there, *Insh' Allah*!'

'*Insh' Allah.* I would like the President to think of me. Serigne Birama, I do not have any secrets with you. A few months ago, the President said he was going to select a Vice-President. Now the rumour goes that he will soon put this into effect. I would like you to pray for the President to think of me.'

'To the Creator, nothing is impossible. All things are in His hands, and He has no other use for all he possesses than to give to His creatures.'

'All that you say to me, I truly believe.'

Mour Ndiaye does indeed truly believe him. Who could have persuaded him that he would ever get to his present position! Oh! those difficult years with the West African Commercial Association, when he could scarcely make both ends meet. When he went about hollow-cheeked and anxious-eyed. When he had only one shirt that he had to wash out overnight and put to dry on the stove in the cold weather. When he had nothing left out of his meagre salary as a copy clerk, after satisfying the pressing demands for money of his parents, cousins, pals, in-laws, who all crowded at the end of every month into the single room that he rented to live with his wife and two children. How distant was this memory! Now he has everything he can wish for: a fine house, two cars at ·his disposal, domestic staff paid for by the State. Sometimes he's worried by his corpulance, especially at official ceremonies when he has to be careful that the buttons of his dinner-jacket don't burst.

The beads of the rosary click. Clack-click-clack. The murmur of Serigne Birama's lips accompanies the music of the beads. Mour is impatient and Serigne Birama's impassive face tells him nothing. He must perforce wait till the rosary is put down on the sheepskin, till Serigne Birama opens his eyes to the light of day, till dialogue is once more established from man to man.

'That which you desire is in God's power to grant you. And I think that He will grant it, *Insh' Allah*. You shall have your wish, if it so pleases God. All you have to do is to sacrifice a fine white ram. You will slaughter it with your own hand; you will divide the meat into seven parts and distribute these to beggars.'

Chapter Four

'They're beginning to make our lives intolerable. Just because we're beggars, they think we're not quite human!'

It is Nguirane Sarr who is speaking. He's fed up with all the persecution. He's got the impression that 'these madmen' have got it in for him especially. And yet he had thought he had won their respect and even their friendship. What had they got against him, when he always stayed quietly at 'his' traffic-lights, never going up to accost people in their cars, knowing that he was dealing with his 'regular patrons' who don't like being disturbed and who give to charity in any case, for their own benefit? And now 'these madmen' don't stop to think any more. They don't make any distinction between people.

'They laid into me today. They tore my clothes, confiscated my stick and broke my glasses. It's too much, it's too much. Is that a way to treat a human being?'

Nguirane is at the end of his tether. Blood is oozing from a cut over his right eye that stretches down to his ear.

'They're quite vicious! When they start laying about them in a fury they're worse than mad dogs.'

All the beggars are afraid now. They are being ceaselessly hunted down without respite. They are afraid and they suffer physically, but that does not stop them from returning to their strategic points every morning; they are drawn back as if by a magnet, armed only with the hope of being able to rely on the speed of their legs to escape from the stinging blows of the policemen's batons, or of hiding in some nearby house when the round-up parties come by.

'But what's got into them all of a sudden? Why this sudden zeal?'

'It's pure bloody-mindedness, that's all.'

They don't understand – and, what is more, who is there to tell them – that they constitute a canker that must be hidden from sight. They have always considered themselves good citizens, practising a trade like everyone else, and because of this they have never tried to define what links them specifically to society. According to them, the contract that links every individual to society can be summed up in the words: giving and receiving. Well then, don't they, the poor, give their blessings, their prayers and their good wishes?

'It's too much, too much,' Nguirane Sarr goes on. 'Since they want war, let it be war.'

'No, Nguirane,' Gorgui Diop replies. 'Don't talk like that. When you beg you have to learn to be patient, to put up with a lot of things. If you need something from someone, you have to satisfy his whims. Besides Nguirane, those who give to us aren't the ones who knock us about.'

Many voices are raised above the general murmurs.

'That's true, that's true. Gorgui Diop's quite right. You have to learn in life not to let a situation get out of hand.'

'Gorgui Diop spoke the truth.'

'Gorgui Diop's words are dictated by reason and wisdom.'

'If we listened to the young we'd be in a nice mess!'

'At any rate, we wouldn't be in our graves,' retorted Nguirane Sarr. 'The young will never lead the way to the cemetery for you. Who was responsible for poor Madiabel's death? Wasn't it those madmen? If they hadn't hunted him down mercilessly, what happened would never have happened.'

Madiabel had died of his injuries. He had lain at the hospital for five days without treatment, because he hadn't a penny on him, and to prove he was a pauper he had to have a certificate from the local authority; and as he was too badly injured to go and get this certificate of indigence which would exempt him from having to pay for treatment, he had lain in a corner, behind a general ward, whose inmates expressed sympathy for his suffering by endless exclamations of 'Ndeisan! Shame! Shame!' whenever he groaned and writhed with the pain that racked him.

The day of his funeral, the whole brotherhood had

accompanied him to his last resting-place and afterwards had collected a quite substantial sum of money to send to his family by way of assistance.

'We're not dogs!' Nguirane Sarr continues. 'Are we dogs, now?'

His voice is shrill with anger and distress and it pierces the thin mist that lightly veils the last glimmer of twilight in the damp air that smells of burning wood. Tiny drops of water form like beads on the copper-coloured faces, expressive of distress and resignation.

'We're not dogs! You know perfectly well we're not dogs. And they've got to be convinced of this too. So we must get organised.'

'How can we get organised? Beggars, get organised! You must be dreaming, Nguirane! You're young! Just leave them to the good Lord.'

'Listen, we can perfectly well get organised. Even these madmen, these heartless brutes who descend on us and beat us up, even they give to charity. They need to give alms because they need our prayers – wishes for long life, for prosperity, for pilgrimages; they like to hear them every morning to drive away their bad dreams of the night before, and to maintain their hopes that things will be better tomorrow. You think that people give out of the goodness of their hearts? Not at all. They give out of an instinct for self-preservation.'

The atmosphere had suddenly grown silent. Ears are pricked up; eyelids flicker, but remain closed. Little by little the mantle of twilight settles on the dark silhouettes which fill Salla Niang's courtyard. She herself stands in the doorway of her room, close to Nguirane. Seeing him so dishevelled, so cast down, at the sight of his face that had been pushed into the dust, and the large gash on his head that gives him the appearance of a martyr, she is filled with compassion. She is indignant. She shares the suffering of this man who she thinks of as her own brother, and who today presents such a downcast appearance. 'Look what they've done to a man who should have deserved some respect, in spite of his poverty.' At the sight of his shirt which has been torn to ribbons, at the sight of a pair of underpants of doubtful whiteness that are visible through the wide rents in what was left of a pair of trousers – now nothing but a collection of rags floating round a semblance of a belt – at the sight of Nguirane's misfortunes Salla Niang has come to the conclusion that there are some forms of suffering that no one has the right to inflict on a human being.

'*Jog jot na! Jog jot na kal!* It's time we did something! It's really time we did something!'

As she speaks she points her right forefinger at the audience. When nobody reacts to this serious warning she goes on, 'It's time we woke up, lads. Nguirane's right. People don't give out of love for us. That's quite correct. So, let's get organised! For a start, don't let's accept any more of those worthless coins they throw us, that won't even buy a lollipop. Eh, my little *talibés*, d'you hear! Spit on their one francs and their two francs; spit on their three lumps of sugar; spit on their handful of rice! D'you hear? Show them we're men as much as they are! And no more prayers for their welfare till we've received a good fat donation! Are you agreed, lads?'

'Ah, *loolu de yomb na*. That's quite easy.'

'Yes, indeed. If one looks into it, what you've just said makes good sense.'

'*Sa degg degg lef li mot naa seetaat*. Yes indeed, we must look into it. Let us do as Salla suggests.'

'Agreed, agreed. We're all agreed.'

They have confidence in Salla. They know she is a woman of experience. She has had plenty of opportunities of getting to know the world. Being orphaned quite young, she had to learn to make her own way in life very early. Her former job as a maid-of-all-work gave her the chance to get to know people, to learn their most intimate secrets and to judge the idiosyncracies of the rich as well as the poor; for she had swept sumptuous villas with their soft mattresses as well as sordid hovels in which at nightfall there were quarrels over a torn pallet whose straw swarmed with bed-bugs. The school of life is probably the best school! You see everything, you get hardened to everything. Nothing surprises you any more, not even a man's most contradictory behaviour.

Salla is now sitting just in front of her door. She rests her elbow on her right knee that is bent up before her; she leans her cheek on her hand.

'They always pretend to look down on the people they need. The last boss I worked for, the one who helped me get this plot of land, spent his time cursing all marabouts. I used to see him on television, I used to hear him on the radio, I recognised his picture in the newspaper when I took it to light the stove. His children explained to me that he wanted to wipe out the curse of the marabouts. He even received some decoration, I think, for his fine speeches. Yes ... when he got his decoration, he organised a grand reception. And yet this man, a real black Frenchman, who drank beer when he was thirsty and whisky when he needed perking up, who only spoke French to his wife and children, well, he never left home in the morning without daubing himself with a mixture of powders and fermented roots that he kept in seven different pots. And those pots gave off such a sickening smell that it made me feel quite ill when I cleaned the bathroom, but it never upset Monsieur. And when he'd finished his speeches, what did he say to the marabouts he put up in his own house? ... Yes, the house was always filled with marabouts; as soon as one left, more arrived with their dirty washing. Oh! their dirty washing! ... Oh! Oh! what a peculiar man that boss was ...'

She had noticed that Monsieur couldn't keep his eyes off her firm breasts. As soon as he got the chance, he'd try a little teasing and then make more definite advances. What a bastard! She had always held out. When Madame was present he didn't even look at her, or else rebuked her harshly on account of a speck of dust on the television or the collar of a shirt that had been badly ironed. Madame intervened and sometimes the matter degenerated into a quarrel.

'Leave the girl alone. She works here, but she's not our slave!'

'Oh! so you dare to question my authority, just over a

servant! One of these fine days I'll give her the sack. And you'll follow her!'

'And then, one day, Madame discovered his little game! The villa was double-storeyed. The bedrooms were upstairs; the lounge, the dining-room and the kitchen were on the ground floor. Monsieur had a weakness for tea; he drank it after lunch and again about six o'clock after work, and again after dinner. Every working day he used to say, 'Salla, keep the last pot of tea for me.' And after his siesta, just before he went back to work, he used to come down to the kitchen while Madame was still resting. He took the opportunity to tease me, to pinch my bottom and fondle my tits. One day – I don't know if she suspected something – Madame suddenly burst into the kitchen while Monsieur was groping and I was trying to escape. We hadn't even heard her approach. When Monsieur caught sight of her standing near the kitchen door, not moving or saying anything, he looked like a man who's had a bucket of ice-cold water thrown over him in mid-winter. He looked shame-faced at Madame who just stood watching him, then he walked over to the table where the teapot was and began to pour the tea into the cups. Madame just stood there for a few minutes, then turned on her heels and left. I never knew if they had it out or not; though I listened with all my ears, I never heard any signs of a quarrel between them and soon afterwards I left the house as I was going to get married.'

After Mour's last visit to Serigne Birama, Lolli had gone back to Keur Gallo to sound out how things were going.

'*Insh' Allah*, this post of Vice-President, he will obtain it. He must sacrifice a bull. He must divide it into thirty-three portions which he must distribute among the poor on a Friday. None of the occupants of his own house must taste the meat. *Insh' Allah*, all will go well.'

Lolli had been hard put to hide her delight. She had let her happiness explode, departing from the reserve that she always maintained before Serigne Birama. For the first time she had raised her voice in the presence of the holy man.

'*Ei Waai amün!* Amen to that! May it please God to do this! *Insh' Allah*, God will not forget us.'

She could already see herself as the wife of the Vice-President of the Republic. What an honour! Naturally, as far as finances were concerned there would be little change. Had she not everything she could hope for? Her wrists were always weighed down with gold and precious stones; her wardrobes were full to bursting; her relatives showered with gifts; she owned three villas bought in her name by Mour Ndiaye because 'you never know in politics; better take all precautions while one can'. But this would be quite different, the prestige of being the wife of the Vice-President! Being so close to the President. Coming just after him! Taking precedence over ministers' wives, over ministers themselves! And everyone making a fuss of her, waiting to carry out her every wish!

And now, were all these dreams to collapse tonight! The night is dark and moonless, quiet and very cold. Mour is in the habit of discussing serious problems with his wife only at times when the whole household is asleep. He places a hand on Lolli's thigh, gives her a soft tap. She stirs; still half asleep she tugs at the blanket.

'Lolli, I've got something very important to tell you. Wake up.'

'Mmm ...'

'Lolli!'

'Yes!'

'I've got to tell you something. Will you please listen carefully to everything I've got to say, and not interrupt me?'

'Yes, I'll listen to you ... Go on, I'm listening.'

'Lolli, you know how much you mean to me. You know I wouldn't exchange you for anything in the world ... I appreciate all your good qualities, your patience, your kindness. Life hasn't always been easy for me; you've put up with all the hardships and difficulties that this has meant for us and you helped me overcome all the obstacles. You're my lucky mascot and you know it.'

'Do you need to tell me all this? I'm your wife and it's

26

normal for me to make your happiness my main concern, for your happiness is mine too. For me, nothing else counts, Mour.'

Lolli means what she says. Her mother had taught her this, and all her aunts, uncles and near and distant relatives had repeated the same refrain and the same recommendations on her wedding-day and again on the night when she moved into the home she was to share with her husband; in a word, on every possible occasion. 'Obey your husband; make his happiness your main concern; on him, your fate and especially that of your children, depends. If you carry out all his wishes, you will be happy here on earth and in the life hereafter, and you will have worthy and deserving children. But, if you don't, then you must expect curses from heaven and the shame of giving birth to children who will turn out failures.' Lolli had always followed this advice. During the first years of their marriage Mour had been liable to frequent indiscretions. He would not come home till nearly dawn and disappear completely for the whole week-end, without ever giving his wife any explanations. Besides, she never asked for any explanations, but she was deeply upset, especially when she was pregnant. On two occasions she had had to wake the neighbours to get them to take her to the nursing-home when her babies were due. When she complained to her parents, they remonstrated with her.

'Lolli, a wife must not grumble. You must understand that your husband is free. He is not an object that belongs to you. You owe him respect, obedience and submission. A wife's sole lot is patience; get that into your head if you want to be a worthy wife.'

So Lolli had said nothing, letting her unhappiness sit heavily on her heart. Then Mour gave the impression of having settled down. Perhaps he had grown tired of running about all night and day. Perhaps, too, he never found another woman as good as his Lolli and realised what a rare jewel he had in her, and that he would be well advised to be satisfied with his lot.

'For me, Mour, nothing counts except your happiness.'

27

'I know, I know. But you've got to understand. In a man's life there are always some unexpected occurrences ... one can't even explain them ... when it has to happen, it just happens.'

'What has happened? What's the matter with you? Are you in trouble?'

Lolli sits up nervously, throws the blanket to the bottom of the bed, switches on the bedside lamp which diffuses a dim light. She is wearing a white nightdress with green dots and an embroidered *beeco* that she pulls down in a vain attempt to cover her thighs.

'No, put your mind at rest ... I only wanted you to know that a man is not completely responsible for his fate ... Everything that happens is fated to happen ...'

'Mour, I can't stand this suspense. Tell me what's the matter. Hurry up!'

Mour is still lying in bed. Out of fear or shame? He cannot meet Lolli's gaze. It seems to him as though her eyes give off sparks. He lights a cigarette to hide behind the smoke. The thought flashes through his mind, like lightning that this woman does not deserve a moment like this. But now that the die is cast, he says to himself, it's too late for this kind of thought. And then, what's so extraordinary about the whole business?

'Mour, please, be quick! Is my father dead? That telephone call just after dinner, was it to say my father was dead? *Wooi*, my father! *Wooi*, my poor father!'

'No, Lolli, there's nothing the matter with your father. Well, this is how it is ... Since you've got to be told, and I want to be the one to tell you myself, out of respect and out of love for you, well, you see ... I'm being given a new wife tomorrow.'

Lolli felt an icy shiver run through her whole body; she felt her teeth chatter and a thick mist clouded her eyes, then, a moment later, she burst out: 'You're "being given" a wife! You prevent me from sleeping! You wake me up in the middle of the night to tell me you're "being given" a wife tomorrow!'

'Lolli, control yourself! Don't shout so loud, you'll wake up the whole neighbourhood ... It'd cause a scandal, especially in the middle of the night!'

Mour seems more at ease now. Though, in his inmost heart he feels his conscience slightly troubling him. After those years spent sowing his wild oats he had learned to appreciate his wife's good points. His numerous affairs had given him the opportunity of seeing the less attractive side of people: women who have no notion of the feminine virtues they are supposed to represent; scenes of uninhibited debauchery; an endless search for sensual pleasures and the artificial paradise of drink and drugs. 'When one has a wife like Lolli, who doesn't make a fool of you, one should keep her safe.' He had arrived at this conclusion over the years, and this opinion was reinforced day by day as he saw her like a cat on hot bricks if the house wasn't properly cleaned, and all the trouble she took to ensure that the children were decently behaved, and how she even supervised their education herself, for though she could neither read nor write she always insisted they sat down with their school books in front of them and she made the older ones hear the younger ones' lessons, and she went regularly to their respective schools to inquire about their behaviour. And those delicious meals that she cooked herself, as a treat for the whole family! Observing his wife day by day had made Mour finally change his attitude towards her and give her the respect she deserved. Moreover, he was very pious; his religious education had left an indelible impression on him; its effects had taken refuge in his subconscious, to reappear on the surface when he was visited by the angel of repentance; then he was filled with remorse and also with fear: he was afraid divine justice would punish him for the suffering he inflicted on this person of flesh and blood who, even in the face of the worst persecutions, the worst humiliations, the worst mental cruelty, never flinched. *Aku jigeen baahul.* Those who ill-treat their wives shall be punished.

Lolli couldn't care less if the neighbours hear her. Let the whole neighbourhood wake up! Let everyone come to their windows in their pyjamas and nightgowns! Let them even come knocking at the door to satisfy their morbid curiosity. What does she care! She has lost all control, because she could have expected anything except this. She had put up with so much and thought that the times of unhappiness and unexpected blows were all over and done with, and now she can't bear this new burden. In earlier times, yes, she might have been able to face it; she would have noted the occurrence with indifference, but now 'times have changed, my lad'.

Lolli's eyes had been opened since she had started going out and about in society. She had seen that women no longer accepted being treated as simple objects. They were engaged in an energetic struggle for emancipation; everywhere, on the radio, at meetings, at family gatherings, they were claiming that, from a legal point of view, they had the same rights as men. Naturally, they were not disputing the man's position as head of the family, but the man had got to realise that his wife is an independent human being, with her own rights and obligations. They were demanding a woman's full right to her full development in the framework of the family, where she should have a voice in all matters, in accordance with her responsibilities. Moreover, they had partly succeeded, as a law had now been passed which henceforward forbade a man from saying to his wife one morning – for no reason at all, simply because he had got out of bed on the wrong side – 'Pack your bags and get out!' Even if the repudiated wife had no home to go to, she had to leave her husband's house and go off to try to find a roof over her head with distant relatives, friends or acquaintances.

Lolli was informed about the campaign for women's liberation that her sisters were waging. Her eldest daughter, Raabi, who was a law student, was always saying, 'Polygamy must be done away with; there's no justification for this practice nowadays.' When she talked like this in noisy discussions with her friends, Lolli had just thought it was the superficial chatter of over-enthusiastic youth. Never had the idea crossed her mind that one day she would have to think seriously about her daughter's words.

'What! And you tell me to keep quiet, into the bargain!
You ungrateful wretch! You bastard, you liar! You want
me to shut up, do you! Twenty-four years of marriage!
You were nothing, nothing but a miserable beggar! And I
backed you up, I put up with everything patiently, I
worked my fingers to the bone, and now you want to
share everything you've got with another woman, thanks
to my patience and my work, and everything that you got
when you married me and that you've got since with my
assistance! You ungrateful wretch, you guttersnipe, you
liar! You men are all the same. Guttersnipe! Shameless
creature! Oh! ... I should have suspected this!'

Lolli's voice carries far; the torrent of her wrath makes
her hoarse and her words come in jerks. Her face bears
the furious expression of a wounded lioness. Her eyes
flash in Mour's face, like those of a wild animal. He can
scarcely recognise her. Whatever has got into her? Mour
decides not to reply to Lolli's insults, preferring to let her
shout till she is tired. Perhaps it will make her feel better.
But soon his masculine pride is aroused and he can no
longer keep quiet.

'That's enough now! I won't allow you to insult me.
You hear, Lolli, I won't allow this; you're carrying things
just a bit too far!'

He has got to his feet now, facing her, his hand raised
threateningly.

'After all,' he goes on, 'just think; I'm the one who
feeds you and keeps you, aren't I? And just tell me what
contract am I tied by that prevents me from taking a
second wife, if I so desire?'

'The contract of decency and gratitude. When you were
nothing, who slaved away? Who wore herself to a shadow
to keep the home going decently on the smell of an oil rag?
Who ran to the marabouts for you? And now, you tell me
something else ... Where did all the money go that my
father and brothers gave me because they were sorry for
me? Into the pockets of marabouts, to unlock the door to
better times for you! And where did all my boubous
disappear to, leaving me only one to my back that I wore
month in, month out? One solitary boubou that in the

end couldn't be distinguished from my skin, so that people didn't say, "That woman there, that's Lolli Badiane", but "That boubou there, that's Lolli Badiane!" In wind and rain and sun, always the same boubou, because the others had all been sold, the same as my bracelets and ear-rings, so that we could keep up some semblance of decency in our lives and not let the children starve. Have you forgotten that already? Ungrateful wretch and liar that you are!'

What can have got into her to put her into such a state and make her speak to her husband as if he were the most despicable of individuals? It is disappointed hopes rather than any indoctrination. Never before had Lolli allowed herself the luxury of any hopes; she had nourished no dreams. She had been long-suffering and had accepted her situation. Then, with the improvement in Mour's treatment of her, and as their political and financial position altered for the better, she was beginning to cultivate some hopes and dreams. And now, Mour waits for the precise moment when all her dreams are possible – 'The Vice-President of the Republic and Madame Ndiaye!' – to inform her that his own happiness can exist apart from his life with her: in fact with a radiant little seventeen-year-old who works as a secretary in a travel agency. Mour had met her at a hotel in a neighbouring country, which he had visited with his Minister, to see what had been accomplished there to develop their tourist sites and clear the cities of their human pollution problem. He had been attracted by her spontaneity, her youth and especially by the ease with which she expressed herself in the official language, with which Mour himself still had some difficulties. She was very elegant and very modern. In order to see her without arousing Lolli's suspicions Mour had invented 'late meetings with V.I.P.s from Europe who were studying the tourist situation', or 'two-day business trips to a neighbouring country', or 'lunches with technical advisers'. Then one day Sine, who had had plenty of time to appreciate her friend's generosity and his love for her, asked him to marry her. 'I'm young and I've all my life in front of me. Marry me or else let me try my luck elsewhere.'

The marriage took place. Raabi tried to convince her mother she ought to fight back, tried to persuade her not to accept the ambiguous situation, telling her it was her duty to prevent an intruder taking her place, that she must 'assume her responsibilities and tell Papa he's got to choose'.

Then Lolli's mother arrived, old Sanou Cissé, with her reputation for virtue and honesty. She burst into tears when Mour told her that Lolli had insulted him and that, if it hadn't been for the children, he would have divorced her. Her father, ill as he was and scarcely able to stand, dragged himself to their house. 'Do you want to be responsible for my death, Lolli? You must know that if Mour divorces you you will be covered with shame. When a woman has got eight children, some of them old enough to be married, she can't allow herself to behave like a child; Mour is your husband. He is free. He doesn't belong to you.'

Her friends also gave her advice: 'You'd be really stupid to lose your husband and let another woman have him. She'd laugh at you and say you were frightened of her.'

'Mother, all these women's arguments are ways of trying to justify themselves. Every one of them would have liked to have a husband to herself; they've all said to themselves, at least once in their lives, that they would never share their husband with anyone. If they haven't said it, at least they've dreamed of it. Then, when they found themselves in the same situation as you are in now, they gave way to the pressures of the old men and women who belong to a different era and can't understand today's world; but they gave way, in the first place, out of cowardice, because they couldn't assume their own responsibilities. Then they tried to find other excuses for remaining in a situation which they really hate. In that way, they thought they were keeping up appearances.'

Raabi is filled with resentment against her father; she knows that her mother is unhappy and that is why she talks to her as a friend. What a child has seen is never forgotten; she can still recall her father's absences, her mother's suffering, the sobs discreetly stifled in the fold of her scarf, then the forced smile to appease the child's questioning gaze. A child of ten guesses everything, and when Raabi was ten, the age when a little girl can take charge of the new baby to relieve Mother a bit, her parents were far from suspecting that they were being watched and judged. Raabi's affection for her mother was infinite; when she reached the age of puberty, Lolli instructed her in her duties as a wife and as Raabi grew more mature the dialogue between them became direct· and frank and they talked together like two friends.

'Raabi, my child, there are things you can't understand. If I left this house today, my parents would curse me, and so would all the members of my family. And if they died, people would say I had killed them by filling their hearts with shame and misery. Think hard, my child; I'd have no work, I'd be all alone, and what would I do with you children if I took you with me? And if I left you here, think how wretched I would be.'

After the storm, resignation. After the first few days spent sulking came renewed efforts to win back the favours of her lord and master. Lolli still nourished one last hope in her heart: that of getting her husband back for herself alone. This was the explanation for confidential discussions with marabouts; this was also the explanation for the exorbitant sums and countless gifts distributed to her in-laws. These must be won over to express their gratitude to her in public, on the occasion of family gatherings, and so giving the impression of swaying the balance in her favour.

Raabi is not convinced. She promises to be rather strong-minded, does Raabi. Lolli sometimes wonders anxiously how her daughter will manage to put up with a husband. She's not pretty, her oval face is rather gaunt, her jaw too prominent, her eyes small and rather hard; she always dresses severely, uses no make-up, wears no useless jewellery, only little hoop ear-rings, a thin chain round her neck, a silver bracelet on her right wrist and a watch on her left wrist. She has never had any time for the trivialities of life; always at her books; interminable

34

discussions with her fellow-students about serious world problems: war, the exploitation of small countries by super-powers, rampant injustice, the dehumanisation of society. She can't stand compromises; she likes clear-cut situations, where you stand up to be counted. That is why she begged her mother not to give way to the countless pressures put upon her; she talked to her as she would to a weak person who doesn't know how to defend her own rights, or hasn't the power to do so. Her mother didn't listen to her, but Raabi does not bear her any ill-will because of this. On the contrary, she understands her motives, but does not consider them justified. This in no way militates against the love she feels for her mother. But when her father returns home, after an absence of four days spent with his 'second', and she sees her mother welcome him like a king, dressed in her best finery, all smiles, incense burning, a meal of delicacies prepared, she is heart-sore. She has no appetite for four long days, during which communication between herself and her father is reduced to formal greetings and short replies to his questions about her studies, her friends or world events.

Chapter Five

The beggars are in a flutter of disquiet; there is a rumble and a grumble of suppressed anger. They have just returned from old Gorgui Diop's funeral. All they knew was that he had been picked up in a raid. A few days later they heard on the radio an announcement from the hospital superintendent, requesting the next-of-kin of Gorgui Diop, deceased, aged about fifty-two, native of Sandiara, to come and collect his body. No one had any idea in what circumstances he had been taken to hospital or what he had died of.

An oppressive silence hangs over Salla Niang's courtyard. It is the moment when the jinn are abroad, wallowing in the heat, when the sun that accompanies the rainy season pierces man's bruised flesh with its flaming darts. Stunned by apprehension and grief, the faces of this human flotsam wear an expression of terror. Tired of being clobbered! Tired of being hunted! Tired of running! For some time now they haven't been going out in daylight any more. They get up before dawn, converge in small tight groups on the markets and the mosques, the only places where human activities are carried on before daybreak. When windows suddenly thrown open to the morning air and the uninterrupted rumble of the traffic announce the awakening of the City, they slip discreetly back to Salla's courtyard.

They have buried old Diop and here they are, back again, heavy-hearted, drenched in perspiration. The scorching air reeks of poverty and human desolation.

'If we don't look out we'll all end up like Gorgui Diop,' Nguirane Sarr cries. 'We'll all die like dogs!'

Today he is wearing a white caftan which has become the colour of ashes. He has bought a new pair of spectacles, this time with black frames. He wears a thin gold chain round his neck. The gash across his face has not yet healed; scabs have formed round the edges of the wound that is stained with mercurochrome.

'And, in any case, Gorgui Diop didn't do anyone any harm,' he resumes.

'Listen, my friends; since they want us to leave them in peace, let's leave them in peace. Let's stay here! Don't let's move from here!'

His friends expected anything but this. They are desperate, terrorised; they want a solution which will ensure that they are treated as citizens with full rights like everyone else. But Nguirane Sarr astonishes them. His suggestion seems devoid of sense.

'We don't go asking for charity any more?'

'What shall we do? Must we be left without any resources? It's true that things aren't easy for us, but we still manage to take a bit of money here and there.'

'Nguirane, your suggestion just isn't feasible. Don't get carried away by anger. Life is full of pitfalls. We must be brave; one day they'll leave us alone. But if we don't go out looking for charity, where shall we go? If we stay at home sulking, we'll just be cutting off our own noses to spite our faces.'

'That's where you're wrong!' Nguirane thunders.

Backs that had stooped beneath the sun's heat are straightened. In Nguirane's voice are undercurrents of hostility, contempt, anger.

'That's where you are wrong! I've told you before: it's not because of our rags, nor our physical disabilities, nor for the pleasure of performing a disinterested good deed that people deign to throw us the money we get as donations. First of all they have whispered their dearest and most secret desires to the alms they tender: "I make you this offering so that God may grant me long life, prosperity and happiness ..." "This donation is so that the Creator may remove all the difficulties I might encounter on my path ..." "In exchange for this contribution may the Master of heaven and earth help me to climb to the top of the ladder, make me the Head of my Department ..." "Thanks to this offering, may the Almighty drive away all my cares as well as those of my family, protect me from Satan, from man-eating sor-

cerers and all the spells that might be cast upon me …"
That's what they say when they drop a coin or a little gift
in the palm of your out-stretched hand. And when they
are kind enough to invite you to share their steaming,
odorous calabashes of millet porridge and curdled milk,
do you imagine it's because they thought you might be
hungry? No, my friends, that's the least of their worries!
Our hunger doesn't worry them. They need to give in
order to survive, and if we didn't exist, who would they
give to? How could they ensure their own peace of mind?
They don't give for our sake; they give for their own
sake! They need us so that they can live in peace!'

Salla Niang, who was cooking the midday meal at the
other end of the courtyard, had been listening to
everything Nguirane had been saying. She now moves
deliberately forward, pushing her way through the dense
throng till she stands in front of Nguirane. She is wearing
a camisole that is pulled in at the waist and shows off the
curves of her hips. Tiny beads of sweat stand out on her
forehead and nose. Gorgui Diop's death has affected her
deeply; she had known him in her native village, where
everyone was unanimous in saying that he had been her
father's best friend. As she had scarcely known her father,
she had transferred all her affection to this man who was
the friend of all the children in the village. Every evening
they crowded round him and he used to tell them
marvellous stories about the origin of the world. Later,
when Salla saw him turn up in the City, she hastened to
offer him her hospitality.

Her features became drawn with sorrow. She reached
out to the assembled crowd a hand stained with henna
arabesques.

'Now, my friends, the hour has come to make our
choice: to live like dogs, pursued, hunted, tracked down,
rough-handled, or to live like men. Gorgui Diop's reason
for living was always to bring a little cheer to men's
hearts. But these madmen have forgotten the meaning of
cheer. Since Gorgui Diop has not been spared – Gorgui
Diop who made people laugh – no one will be spared. So
now, let's have no more of this stealing in and out on the

sly; let's have no more of this running away like mad; let's have no more distress and fear. Let's all stay here! Do you hear, we'll stay here! In a very short time you'll see that we are as necessary to them as the air they breathe. Where will you find a man who's the boss and who doesn't give to charity so that he can stay the boss? Where will you find a man who's suffering from a real or imaginary illness and who doesn't believe that his troubles will disappear the moment a donation leaves his hands? Where will you find an ambitious man who doesn't think that the magic effects of charity can open all doors? Everyone gives for one reason or another. Even the parents of a man who's awaiting judgement, expecting to be condemned, have recourse to charity, to blur the judge's reasoning, in the hope of an acquittal.'

Everything that Salla Niang has said is based on what she saw during her experiences as a maid-of-all-work. She lived in houses where everyone stuffed themselves fit to burst; the left-overs that they threw in the dustbin could have fed ten paupers, but paupers were never invited to share the meal; paupers are dirty, a nuisance, they don't know how to behave. But, in these same houses, when the marabout recommended them to feed seven, ten or twelve paupers on delicacies for three days, they went to seek out these same paupers, invited them to their homes, welcomed them, pressed dishes upon them that they would never have dreamed of: rice with fish, swimming in a rich, red sauce; white rice with plenty of tender meat; a delicious couscous with raisins, mixed vegetables, dates and prunes; and after every meal, fresh cola-nuts to aid the digestion.

What Salla Niang has just said is not the result of a sudden inspiration. It derives, among other experiences, from a painful scene which she witnessed at a time when she worked for some people who were not exactly rolling in money. As she made the beds, swept the rooms, scoured the saucepans, she kept her ears and eyes open and so was able to reconstitute the drama in which the family was involved. The husband, Galaye, was leader of the workers' union in a small metalworks, whose owner didn't look very favourably on the union's demands which, he said, were 'an obstacle to good working conditions and liable to have disastrous consequences for the financial situation of the firm'. The owner's motto was 'The output first, foremost and all the time' and this motto had become a sort of regular prayer recited at all times of the day, accompanying the showers of sparks given off from the welders' oxyacetylene lamps. To justify his obsession, he invoked the heavy taxes he had to meet, although all his employees knew that he enjoyed the enormous facilities and tax concessions granted to foreign investors. The workers' rights and the most elementary safety regulations no longer counted, and it became Galaye's duty to remind him that there were bye-laws relating to the employees' conditions of work. The owner did not appreciate Galaye's submissions and gave him to understand that under no circumstances was his firm – which had been set up to help the State and the workers – to be transformed into a political forum.

'You're here to get on with your work and not to create trouble! If you don't want to work, you can bugger off! There are hundreds waiting for your job!'

'If anyone here ought to bugger off, it's you! This is our country, and that's what you seem to forget! You just comply with the regulations laid down in the bye-laws; just pay us the overtime you owe us; and see that there's soap in the washrooms after work! And we must ask you again to install at least two fire-extinguishers. In a firm like this, it's inconceivable that there isn't a single one!'

While these exchanges were being shouted above the shrill hiss of the oxyacetylene lamps in the workshop, most of the welders remained bent over their jobs.

'That's right, Mister Galaye, go on! And while you're at it, why don't you demand air-conditioners to diminish the effects of the heat!'

That had been the end of the argument that day. But Galaye had no idea how far his employer would go in double-dealing. The latter had got the impression that the factory ran the risk of being at the mercy of a wave of rebellion which would seriously impair his profits. To enable him to sack Galaye without paying him any compensation, he got some of the latter's compatriots to aid and abet him by dazzling them with wild promises of advancement. One day he pointed out to the storeman that the chit authorising the removal of ten wrought-iron gates from the workshop was a forgery. The storeman submitted that the chit had been given to him by Galaye. The owner brought a charge against Galaye who denied his guilt, but the storeman persisted in his accusation. Finally Galaye was condemned to three months' imprisonment, with suspended sentence, plus costs and the repayment of the value of the ten gates, estimated at sixty thousand francs each.

Galaye was out of work for a long time. While Salla Niang took care of the housework, his wife made pagnes and prepared fritters which she sold to meet the family's expenses.

One morning, very early, Salla saw Galaye take a bench and place it in front of the entrance to the house. He sat there, holding a sheet of white paper in his hand. Salla watched him out of the corner of her eye as she lit the stove, and could not explain his apparent nervousness. As usual beggars streamed past but Galaye remained deaf to their pleas for alms.

This intrigued Salla all the more. Finally an old beggar-woman came past; she was tiny, wrinkled, but bright-eyed. On her head she carried two little calabashes placed one on top of the other, and ash-grey strands of hair escaped from her tightly-knotted head-scarf. As soon as Galaye caught sight of her he ran up to her and offered her the white paper saying, 'Take this, lady, it's a gift from God!'

The old beggar-woman, who presumably found this a rather odd gift, showed her surprise; she frowned and looked carefully to make sure there was nothing in the paper. Galaye's hand trembled as he held it out. Salla watched, her broom in her hand.

'It's charity, Grandma! I'm giving it you out of charity!'

'Eh, son! What can I do with a piece of paper? I can't read or write!'

41

She continued to hold her two calabashes on her head with both hands. She seemed to have no inclination to take the paper.

'Beggars can't be choosers! That's a divine law! It says you mustn't pick and choose and you mustn't look a gift-horse in the mouth!'

'Perhaps you're right, my son. But a piece of paper ...'

She was about to turn away. Salla saw Galaye pleading with her, imploring, beseeching with burning eyes and parched throat. The old beggar-woman remained unmoved and tried to go on her way. Then Galaye caught hold of her camisole, dug his hand into his pocket and brought out a shining coin which he waved under the woman's nose.

'Take the paper and take this money too.'

Salla thought to herself that Galaye was certainly parting with the last money he had left. She felt quite heart-sore. Later, as she listened to conversations through the wall, she learned that Galaye had been told by a marabout that it was essential for him to give this sheet of paper to an old woman in order to obtain a job.

Chapter Six

'You must be pleased now! The street corners are deserted; there's not a single beggar to be seen any more.'

There is a semi-reproachful note in Sagar Diouf's voice as she speaks to Keba. The latter was just drifting into a daydream, intoxicated by the sea air that he breathes deeply into his lungs, by the sight of the monotonous landscape of the coast which glides past the car, by the enchantment of the music broadcast by the radio: in this duet of contrasting voices which seem to range into infinity and lose themselves in the depths of one's soul, accompanied by the melancholy sobbing, drawn from the *Kora* by skilful fingers, Keba recognises Soundiou Sakho and his wife, the celebrated singing couple who have the strange power of flexing the most rigid strings and touching the coldest hearts.

'What power, what sweetness, what magic in these voices! You see, Sagar, every time I hear them, I feel as if I'm losing a little of my bodily presence, while I am filled with an ineffable happiness.'

'What voices?' Sagar asks.

She has not noticed the music. She is waiting impatiently to discover the new hotel complex on the Lower Coast, a veritable paradise, according to what is said in the Capital, and where Keba has invited her this weekend.

'But … the sound of the kora and the voices of the singers!'

'Oh! … I was saying there are no more beggars in the City. You've succeeded? I forgot to ask you: is it true the President is very pleased and that because of this he's going to appoint Mour Ndiaye to the new post of Vice-President?'

'I don't know. There is a rumour to this effect in the City, but Mour Ndiaye hasn't said anything to me.'

'You can be sure that if he is appointed Vice-President,

you'll be the new Minister! I really, sincerely hope so, for your sake. After all, it's you who've done all the work.'

'I did it because it's my job, not because I expected any promotion. Besides the problem of the beggars is so important for me that I would have asked to take it on personally if chance had placed me in another Department.'

Sagar bursts out laughing again. When she mentioned the problem of the beggars, she expected this passionate and almost childish reaction from Keba. The vein stands out on his forehead; his expression which a moment ago was calm, is now tense. Just because of a silly business of a few beggars; Sagar will never understand Keba's motives.

'What attracts you towards the beggars? They're poor; aren't you sorry for the poor?'

'What attracts me towards the beggars! You're wrong, Sagar, you never see anything! You never understand anything! Don't you realise that everything separates me from them! Poverty has never compelled people to beg; poverty has never excluded self-respect, human dignity! I've told you this a thousand times!'

Sagar does not reply. The amused smile which lit up her face has disappeared. She has perceived in Keba's voice and expression something that she has never noticed before: as if he felt a deep suffering that he was repressing with a supreme effort. She is all the more surprised in that she thought that in this hour of success Keba could not help being happy. She stares at him: in his eyes that are fixed determinedly on the tarred road that unfurls before them, a red veinule has appeared; his lips are tightly closed and the pulse throbs feverishly on his prominent temples. The silence is broken only by the uninterrupted hum of the motor and the whistle of the salt-laden breeze that bends the tops of the coconut palms that line the road. The car is travelling more slowly now: Keba glances briefly at Sagar and makes an effort to relax his lips in a forced smile.

'Sagar, don't be cross with me; it's not you I'm angry with, but those people who do a real wrong to humanity, and who, if you look carefully, harm the genuinely poor, that is the ones who have nothing but who manage to keep up an appearance of respectability and dignity ...'

At the side of the deserted road a group of children can be seen from time to time, with bare chests, their hair reddened by the sun and the sea; they give broad, innocent smiles and wave their hands in greeting.

'When I was a boy, I saw a striking example of unselfishness on the part of a woman who was never reduced to begging, by either hunger or extreme poverty ... I saw a family – are you listening, Sagar? – I saw with my own eyes what I'm going to tell you – I didn't hear it from anyone. A family of five children, the husband drowned one day when he went out fishing in a home-made canoe; the wife was paralysed in the right arm and depended on the small allowance that one of her brothers who was a school-teacher grudgingly gave her, and on the meagre proceeds from the sale of roast peanuts, which was the only way she could earn anything, because she was handicapped by her useless arm. One holy day she paid a visit to her brother, accompanied by her five children, all boys. Her brother had three wives and a large number of children. This large family, together with many people who had come to present the compliments of the season, were sitting in the spacious courtyard round the master of the house. The woman – her name was Dibor – greeted him and mingled with the crowd of people present, while her children ran off to find their young cousins. The master of the house then called two of them in a disagreeable, dictatorial voice, "Hey, you there, Birama, Famara, come here!"

'The two children pushed forward and stood in front of their uncle. The latter then called one of his own sons, Talla. All the people present watched them. The master of the house shouted, "Birama, Talla tells me that you and your brother steal pens every day at school. You little hooligans, isn't everything I do for you enough?"

'The children denied the charge, with their eyes lowered. The woman got up from where she sat and shouted at her brother in an unaccustomed fury, "Bougouma, that's a low-down thing to do. That's not the way a human being behaves; anyone would think you were speaking to a dumb beast! It's wicked to want to shame children in front of everyone, simply on the basis of your son's accusations. Is your son any better than them? Doesn't the same blood flow in their veins? What a petty way to behave! How petty to expend so much energy over a trifling matter of a few miserable pens! I'll have you know, Bougouma, that all I've got to live on is what you give me and what I earn from my roast peanuts, but God hasn't yet deprived me of the means of buying pens for my children. Your son is a liar and you encourage him!''

'After this furious outburst, Dibor called her children and left her brother's house where she never set foot again, while the people who had gathered in the courtyard blamed her for having spoken in this way to her brother who was also her benefactor. Bougouma cut off her allowance and they had no further contact.'

Keba did not tell Sagar that his mother wept ceaselessly all that night and that he – the Birama of the story – swore that he would never forgive his uncle and that one day he'd get his own back for this public insult inflicted on him, on account of some miserable pens. And he kept his word: the uncle was pensioned off after having invested all his savings to build the house where he lived with his large family. Then he was expropriated because he had built on a site that belonged to the state; the meagre sum that was offered him in compensation could not begin to counterbalance all the outlay he had had for his house. Then he remembered his nephew who might intervene with the Minister on his behalf. As soon as he had one foot inside Keba's office and the other still outside, elated and proud to be the uncle of a man who was respected and praised everywhere in the Capital, he was greeted by a face like a thundercloud and a terrifying roar which stopped him dead in his tracks, with one foot inside the door and the other outside, unable either to open or close it. 'Get out! I refuse to see you! Out, you understand, out!'

Sagar gets the impression that the road has got busier

now with the peasants returning home in their short trousers, their backs bent, carrying farm instruments on their shoulders. Women walk along with huge loads of sticks or enormous baskets on their heads.

'Poverty', Keba resumes, 'is always heart-breaking, but it's impossible to imagine the hardships that family subsequently endured. Five mouths to feed, children who don't understand and pull a long face at the sight of boiled rice, without any sugar, because the grocer on the corner won't allow any more credit. And the mother who kept her self-respect, grimly refusing to beg, to ask for anything, but obliged – because of the children, only because of the children – to accept the left-overs from neighbours' tables or the reach-me-downs that they offered them out of pity.'

'So she did accept charity!' Sagar exclaimed. 'And you admired her for it!'

'She never held out her hand to ask for anything, Sagar! That's very important. What I admired about her was her strength, her will-power in resisting the temptation of making a show of her suffering and her hunger. It was her refusal to give other creatures no better than herself the opportunity of snubbing her, and treating her as someone undesirable. It's incredible, if you imagine that there were some periods of total indigence when the cooking pot that she placed on the fire in the evening – made from a few twigs that she had collected – contained nothing but water. The children waited. 'The cassava's very hard today, it'll soon be soft.' And the children waited hopefully; she told them stories and sang them the songs that used to excite the wrestlers in the arena in the olden days. Finally they fell asleep. Only the oldest one, Birama, knew that the cooking-pot contained nothing but water.'

Sagar hasn't even been listening to Keba's last words; it is enough for her to observe once again that Keba is a rather peculiar person, who doesn't react like other people. She remembers the day she had asked him for some petrol vouchers.

'What do you want petrol vouchers for? To the best of

my knowledge you don't own a car.'

'It's for one of my friends. She works in the private sector and it's not always easy for her to get them.'

'All right. Bring your friend here.'

When Sagar and her friend were seated in front of Keba, expecting some grand gesture on the part of a generous boss, Keba turned to the friend whom Sagar had introduced to him a few moments before.

'Mademoiselle Dieng, I understand that you want some petrol vouchers.'

'Yes, sir.'

'What make of car have you got?'

'A Peugeot 504.'

'How did you purchase it?'

'Why ... with my own money!'

Up till then Sagar had been under the impression that they had just been making conversation, although this was not in Keba's nature. 'But who knows? Perhaps today he's feeling in a particularly light-hearted mood.'

'So you've got enough money to buy yourself a car!'

Silence.

'Well, Mademoiselle, I'm sorry, but since you yourself offer me the opportunity, I'll take advantage of it to draw your attention to certain very important matters which may well have escaped you, because you simply haven't thought about them ... Well then: first of all, don't you think it is degrading to ask for things? And then, one must be prepared to assume one's responsibilities; if one buys a car, one must be in a position to buy petrol, for before buying your car you knew that it can't work without fuel! Finally, Mademoiselle, you know very well that the petrol vouchers you are asking me for don't belong to me; they belong to the State. In asking me for them, you are inciting me to rob the State; do you think that is honest?'

Sagar had felt the ground literally giving way under her; she was paralysed with shame and could find no other outlet than to burst into tears. But Mademoiselle Dieng was by no means put out; she stood up, placed her handbag and her large glinting spectacles on Keba's desk, pulled her blouse down over her skirt and snapped her fingers at him.

'You're out of date! And you're too young to try to teach me how to act. Since your coupons are so precious, you can stuff them! Stuff them, my lad, my car will go on running! Sagar, your boss is crackers!'

After this scene Sagar had every intention of leaving Keba's department as soon as she could, and then time had sorted things out; she had come to the conclusion that Keba was different from other people and that one had to accept him as he was.

Chapter Seven

Mour Ndiaye has been awarded the Order of Merit, an honour which is reserved for nationals who have shown quite exceptional qualities. He is the second citizen to be able to glory in the rare title of Knight of the Order of Merit, the first being Lieutenant-Colonel Massaer Sarr, who was decorated for succeeding in breaking up the celebrated network of smugglers who deprived the State every year of hundreds of millions and who, till then, had constituted a national scourge that no one had been able to eradicate. After his decoration, Lieutenant-Colonel Massaer had been appointed Minister of Finance and Commerce, which is an added reason, on top of the rumours which continue to be current and the compliments which the President heaps upon him, for confirming Mour Ndiaye's hopes of being appointed Vice-President. He has more extensive and more frequent contacts with marabouts. Mour is no longer satisfied to consult the most esteemed marabouts of his own country; he travels through foreign territories and sends his confidential agents into quite distant lands in search of the greatest specialists in occult science.

Congratulated everywhere for having finally cleaned up the streets, the market-places, the traffic-lights at the intersections, the pavements in front of the big shops, hospitals, banks and hotels, Mour eventually esteems himself the heaven-sent individual to whom the whole nation should pay tribute. He has assumed an air of complacency, he gives dinner after dinner and reception after reception in order to hear himself congratulated by the social elite. He isn't just Mour Ndiaye any more, he is 'that exceptional man who succeeds in rectifying compromising situations'; he has become one with his own image of himself.

One day, however, Mour comes down to earth again after a night of terrifying dreams. Troubled by these, he goes to ask counsel of one of his many marabouts who instructs him to make an offering of seven white cola-nuts to an old woman who has no physical infirmity. 'Be particularly careful not to give them to a blind woman!'

How great is his disappointment, his distress, his fear also, when his son brings back the cola-nuts, explaining that he hasn't seen a single beggar! Mour is vexed, but to tell the truth he is afraid that this is an unlucky omen: will this terrible nightmare which has so upset him, and which must be exorcised by giving away the colas, come true because the colas have come back? He falls into a terrible rage.

'You good-for-nothing! You're all a lot of ne'er-do-wells. You're not even capable of going out and giving alms to a beggar!'

'But papa, I did try. I went ever so far and I didn't see a single beggar!'

'You're lying. Now go and find someone to give those nuts to! If you bring them back you'll see what stuff I'm made of. Go on, you lazy-bones!'

Just when his son is about to leave, Mour calls him back. 'No, leave it alone. Give them to me!'

He calls one of the servants. 'Sally, here's a thousand francs for you. Try to find an old woman who's not lame, who's not blind, not even in one eye, and give her these colas. Don't bring them back under any circumstances, Sally. This donation must be made today, urgently.'

Sally explored the whole district without meeting a single beggar. In any case, it is common knowledge this district has never suffered from the continuous assault of beggars. The only establishment that risked being frequented is the baker's shop, and the baker some time ago – long before the mopping-up campaign – had taken care to clear his shop of these undesirable canvassers of all sorts: beggars, hawkers, shoe-shine-boys and others.

'I've got my washing-up to do … and the laundry … it's getting late … what must I do with these cola-nuts …?'

Sally gives way to the temptation simply to throw them away to get rid of them; she places them at the foot of a tree and goes away. Then, feeling a pang of remorse just as she is slipping the thousand-franc-note, folded in four, into her brassière, she turns round quickly, picks up the cola-nuts wrapped in a piece of white paper, stands for a moment with them poised in her hand, not knowing what she must decide to do. Fortunately she catches sight of a bus.

'It can't be helped! I'd better go to the Main Market ... The washing up ... The laundry ... If I take the bus, it won't take me too long.'

She explores the whole market. For want of beggars, she has recourse to examining the multicoloured objects that glitter on the merchants' stalls. She bargains hard and buys a pair of ear-rings, some gilt bracelets and a jar of skin-lotion. Just as the stallkeeper is passing her her parcel, she is once more aware of the weight of the colas.

'Brother, do you know where the beggars hang out?'

'Hi-i-i-! Don't you live in the City?'

'Yes, of course, I live here!'

'Then you don't know what's happening? It's not easy now to meet a beggar; you never see them any more; they don't come to get their handout; people take it to them.'

'Where?'

'It's a long way out, you know! In the new Slum-Clearance Resettlement Area.'

Sally counts her money. Out of the thousand francs that Mour gave her, she has a hundred and forty francs left. She hasn't the heart to go back without having deposited the nuts in the hands of an able-bodied old beggar-woman. 'The washing-up ... The laundry ... But the master treats me so well ...'

'People are really in the soup now,' the stallkeeper went on. 'They're short of beggars. Can you imagine an existence in which you can't make your daily offering to charity without travelling several miles?'

Sally gets on the bus again. When she gets off at the stop which has already been christened 'the beggars' bus-stop', she has no difficulty in finding Salla Niang's house; all she has to do is to follow the crowds that converge on it from all directions, carrying diverse packets. To listen to the conversations exchanged, the complaints at having to travel so far to make their donations, she realises that the shortage of beggars is causing a considerable inconvenience to a part of the population; she sees sick people, pale and haggard, who have dragged their suffering this distance in order to make the sacrifice which may perhaps help them to be restored to physical and mental well-being. She sees luxurious cars, with all their windows tightly closed, speeding down the sandy track that leads to 'the beggars' house'. She hears the laments of people of modest means who condemn the ever-increasing demands of the beggars: 'They really go too far! They don't care a damn for what the Holy Scriptures lay down. Can you imagine their cheek! The amount prescribed for a donation is seven lumps of sugar or a candle, and here are these ladies and gentlemen demanding to be offered anything up to two pounds of sugar or a really thick blanket that's not been patched. And they are the ones who decide what they'll have! And you can't please them so easily; they have to have the best … But what can we do?'

Chapter Eight

In his New Year speech to the Nation, the President of the Republic spoke of his optimism about the future of the country; he announced a period of prosperity and encouraged all the citizens to persevere in their efforts for the good of the State. He quoted the example of Mour Ndiaye, who by his skilful, intelligent and firm handling of the problem, has succeeded in ridding the Capital of a nuisance, thus favouring the progress of tourism, which in turn has been responsible for the considerable rise in the standard of living of the citizens, since the average income per capita has undergone a substantial increase.

The new congratulations publicly addressed to Mour Ndiaye by the President in the same speech, moreover, which confirmed his intention of reshuffling the cabinet and appointing a Vice-President of the Republic in the near future, constitute in everyone's eyes the proof that Mour will shortly be promoted and his Minister of State removed from office. Moreover the latter has been waging an open war against Mour for some time. At every opportunity, in the course of receptions, political conventions, meetings of sectional committees, he never fails to remind people that Mour has undoubtedly a bent for politics, in the popular sense of the term; that he has the knack of mobilising the masses; but that he has no training which would qualify him for any claim to be able to take charge of the Government. 'He can't even express himself correctly in the official language of the country, so how could he take on this function?' To the many questions asked by the embittered Minister, certain people replied ironically, 'And what pray are technical advisers for?'

When this malicious talk reached Mour's ears, he was not unduly hurt. He saw in it the pique and mortification of a man who has known the delights of high honours, who has wallowed in them without thought for the morrow, and who knows he is about to be tumbled from his tower. Mour has never paid any particular attention to the Minister's sniggers, nor those of his cronies; he has simply asked his marabouts to protect him from all the spells that might be woven against him and to help him obtain the coveted post of Vice-President of the Republic as rapidly as possible. Mour is fully aware that many other people in high positions in the country are scheming to get this post. That is why, after having been advised by Serigne Birama to pray to God and wait calmly and with equanimity for the glory with which the Creator would soon surround him, he went off to a pastoral village in the heart of the bush, which is reputed for the infallible knowledge of its marabouts. He returned accompanied by the man who for miles and miles around is considered to be the one whom no forces can resist. He is said to converse with *jinn* and that they in turn carry out all his wishes, even the ones that seem the most impossible to realise. No one has ever seen his face which he always keeps hidden beneath a *chéchia*, which leaves only his little red eyes visible with a gaze as sharp as a steel blade. He is known to everyone by the curious name of Kifi Bokoul for the following reason: The story goes that his mother was for long completely barren. Neither powders, nor potions nor incantations sung in pitchblack night in the heart of the deserted bush succeeded in satisfying her desire to bear a child. And yet there was nothing of the harridan about her: she was kindness itself. One day, she had gone with her husband to the foot of the fetish-tree of her village; her husband implored the spirits with tears in his eyes to come to the help of his wife who, in seventeen years of marriage, had never raised her eyes to look him in the face and had always carried out his most capricious requests. For this model wife, the husband had offered the spirits gold dust, camel's milk and steaming bull's blood in the cool of the early dawn. After this sacrifice, an enormous snake had glided down from the tree and had addressed the couple in these words: 'A child will be born from the entrails of this woman, a child whose eye will be able to perceive what you will never see. For this being whom this woman will bear, will be born of you, he will live among you, but he will not be one of you.' When the snake had pronounced these obscure words it ordered the woman to dance; she had danced and danced and danced until she fell into a trance and then fell sound asleep; then her husband lifted her on to his sturdy shoulders and they returned home. Shortly afterwards the child who was to bear the name of Kifi Bokoul was conceived.

Mour Ndiaye took Kifi Bokoul home to Lolli's house, as he had done with so many other marabouts. For Sine, the second wife, was still being coddled and given everything that she desired; but Lolli is the depository of all Mour's secrets regarding his dealings with marabouts. He is convinced that whatever happens Lolli will never betray his secrets, for this would be out of keeping with the pattern of behaviour which has been laid down for her; and it so happens that she has been so conditioned that she will never permit herself any departure from this pattern. The proof of this is that after the stormy reaction to Mour's second marriage, she resigned herself to accepting her new situation. Lolli will never permit herself any deviation from the accepted standards; even the one little escapade that she had once been guilty of only helped to assure her place within the accepted pattern of behaviour: it was the innocent enough occasion when all the girls from the district ran away in search of a tattooist in a neighbouring village. She left her parents' house without letting anyone know, but when they realised that all the adolescent girls had disappeared, they understood; they felt immensely happy and proud that they had managed to inculcate into their daughter the indispensable virtue of *jom*, which constitutes a restraint on any reprehensible behaviour. And with the other parents they made ready to honour the girls who had gone to brave pain; they prepared enormous quantities of couscous and decided on the bull which would be slaughtered for the festivities organised to welcome them when they returned from the trials of the tattooing. And one day, at the entrance to the village, the beat of tom-toms was to be heard and all the inhabitants of the village ran to meet the initiates: their lower lips and chins were all indigo stained, and they danced to the rhythm of the tom-toms, to songs and the happy clapping of hands, while the tattooist who accompanied them back sang their praises and received many gifts from all the villagers. All the young men were also at the feast; and this was the first time that Mour had been struck by Lolli Badiane's physical appearance: tall as a gazelle, fresh as a sea-breeze, as she returned from the only escapade that could be tolerated – an honourable escapade.

Chapter Nine

Kifi Bokoul remained shut up for seven days and seven nights in the guest apartment of Lolli's house, eating nothing but couscous sprinkled with lukewarm water which was placed every evening, just before bed-time, outside the door of the apartment, as no one must see the marabout during his retreat. After seven days and seven nights, which seemed to Mour to last for centuries, Kifi Bokoul gave his verdict:

'You will have what you desire, and you will have it very shortly. You will be Vice-President. To achieve this, you must sacrifice a bull whose coat must be of one colour, preferably fawn. The ground must be soaked with the blood of this bull which you must slaughter here in the courtyard of this house; then you must divide it into seventy-seven portions which you will distribute to the *bàttu*-bearers.'

'What are the *bàttu*-bearers?' Mour asked.

'They are beggars who walk about the streets to beg. This offering must go to its correct destination, otherwise everything risks going wrong. It must go to genuine *miskin*, that is to genuine paupers, people who have nothing, absolutely nothing and who would starve, were it not for their *bàttu* that they stretch out to passers-by. You have heard my words?'

'I have heard and I have fully understood; everything shall be done as you say.'

'But this sacrifice that you will make, must not be limited to one district of the town only. You are destined to be appreciated in the four corners of the town, in the four corners of the country; you will be a man of fame; this fame must be symbolised by the manner in which you distribute the meat from the sacrifice: offer this meat throughout the City, to the beggars in every district of the City.

'*Insh' Allah*, Serigne. *Insh' Allah* I shall follow your

recommendations ... And when I have done all this, I shall obtain what I desire? ...'

'Those who know me know that my words have never been wasted on the empty air.'

'That is true. That is true Serigne ... Forget that I mentioned it.'

'If you make the offerings as indicated, with three times seven yards of white, non-silky material, as well as seven hundred cola-nuts, of which three hundred must be red and four hundred white, you will be Vice-President a week later. Not later than a week.'

Mour thrills with happiness. He gazes at Kifi Bokoul as if to try to pierce his mystery, but all he can see is a little, shrivelled wisp of a man, huddled on a sheepskin which is quite large enough to serve him as a bed, the way he is curled up on it. His whole body is wrapped in his blue cotton boubou, and when Mour makes so bold as to try to descry the minutest fragment of something in this head resting on a hand which is entirely hidden beneath the boubou, he comes up against two tiny, mobile, apparently bottomless apertures behind the chéchia which is disproportionately voluminous in comparison with the man's diminutive silhouette.

'This man is certainly quite extraordinary; he isn't human ... no, he isn't human ... A week after the sacrifice ...'

'If you make the offerings as indicated, and you are not appointed a week later, you can spit on my chéchia, you can drag me in the mire, you can take my life if you so wish.'

After this interview, when the retreat of seven days and seven nights had elapsed, Kifi Bokoul took his leave of Mour. The latter asked Kouli, the most loyal of his chauffeurs, to drive him back to his village, then he began to cogitate on the words of 'this man who is not human'. And suddenly he recalled that the beggars no longer beg in the streets; he has purged the streets of them and forced them to take refuge somewhere in a corner of one of the outlying districts.

'Sally! Sally!'

'Yes, sir ...'

'The other day, where did you take the colas to?'

'A long way away, sir. In the beggars' house.'

'Ah! ... They have a house?'

'Yes, in the new Slum-Clearance Resettlement Area. That's where everyone goes to find them and make their donations to charity. The day I took the colas, I went by bus.'

'Good, that's all right. You can go.'

The beggars are living like princes; they are even beginning to get bored at having nothing to do from morning to evening. Donations rain from heaven and lately they have noticed greater crowds and more generous gifts: Salla Niang's shop has benefited from a stock of meat where all the inhabitants of the neighbourhood come to make their purchases of excellent quality cuts. One day, Nguirane Sarr, who now plays the guitar to fill in his excess of leisure time, suddenly interrupted his recital and said to his fellow-beggars, 'I'm sure that something is happening in the world of politics! All this activity, all these luxury cars driving up the whole day, these fine horned rams ... that can only be because of politics.'

'No, the radio would have mentioned it ... The radio hasn't said anything about elections ...'

'You see,' says Nguirane, 'I was right. Now, all we have to do is to sit down and everything falls from heaven. We don't have to go out early in the morning any more, we don't have to keep on the run all the time, we don't have to strain our vocal chords any more, shouting above the noise everywhere.'

'It was hard, very hard. And to think that if it weren't for you, Nguirane, we would have gone on with this disastrous game of hide-and-seek with those people who were hounding us, and we should have gone on getting the worst of it.'

'The mistake they made', Nguirane goes on, 'was never to stop to think why we begged.'

'Do people stop to ask that kind of question? Really,

Nguirane, sometimes you talk as if you were dreaming! Why were we begging? The answer's easy, we begged because we had nothing!'

'No! I say we begged because we couldn't work because of our physical infirmities.'

'If we begged, it was because every individual doesn't have the same opportunities, and those people who are better off must give some of their wealth to the poorer ones. That's what religion says: when we beg we just claim what is our due!'

Nguirane lets his fellow-beggars argue about the various reasons why they are beggars; then, when silence has been restored, he says, 'Certainly opportunities are not the same for everyone! You see my cousin who often comes to see me here, he has done a lot of studying, he's a "situdent" in the biggest school in the City and soon he'll be a "dokatari" if God wills; he'll look after the sick.'

'Is that so? If I'd known that I'd have shown him my sores and I'd have asked him to give me a medicine! Oh! how I itch, how I itch!'

'Hey Nguirane, tell him to help me to get to hospital. My child has been sick for long enough, anyone would think! He coughs and vomits his heart out. I put him on my back, I take the bus to the hospital, but they won't let me in. They ask me for a paper from the nurse here at the clinic. Three times I've been there and back for nothing and the child's getting weaker by the hour!'

'That cousin', Nguirane resumes, 'grew up with me in our village. His father and my mother have the same mother. Before I lost my sight we went to the Koranic school together ...'

'Oh, so you weren't born blind?'

'No, when I was struck with this infirmity I was already a sturdy lad; it was the result of an illness ... I studied with the same marabout as my cousin; we both went to beg for our food; we went from door to door, calling out in our shrill voices, and the people who were not well-off in the village still gave us a little share of what they had ...'

'The city changes people ... It lures them in and destroys them ...'

61

'Begging', Nguirane continues, 'was not considered a curse then. It was quite natural for those who found themselves obliged to beg, and it was considered a duty for those who gave ...'

'Nguirane! You are too fond of holding forth! You're only happy when you're palavering!

'Salla, go away and look after your cooking-pot. Today we want a really juicy couscous, hey! I hope you've put the tripes and the head in. If the sauce isn't rich enough I'll tell your "uncle" who'll put you in your place!'

Everybody bursts out laughing. Salla just shakes her head and smiles while she continues cleaning her teeth with a piece of *sump*-root.

'And then, one day', Nguirane resumes, 'my cousin was sent to school; meanwhile I had lost my father and was plunged into the blackness of an endless night; my mother who couldn't maintain me put me in the care of a marabout who lived in the neighbourhood. Even if I hadn't been blind, how could I exercise a trade, when I hadn't learned anything, and I hadn't been trained for anything?'

'But you have got a trade! You are a beggar!'

Nguirane does not reply to this pleasantry which comes from the other end of the vast courtyard, filled with men and women of all ages.

'My cousin, thanks to the schooling he received, and thanks to the intelligence which God gave him, was able to come out all right. And *we* thought we'd survive by coming to the City which we saw in our dreams as a paradise where nothing was lacking ...'

'Really, Nguirane, you're never satisfied. What more do you need now? Before, you had to go out to beg, sometimes people snubbed you, other times they gave you something; then they started hunting you down like a mad dog; now you stay here and you've got people coming to you bringing everything you need here: clothes, food, money. What more do you want? D'you think that the workers have got as much?'

'Salla, I'm not complaining. Even my cousin said that we've got nothing to complain about and that we ought to have adopted this attitude a long time ago. When he comes here and sees people besieging us, he has a good laugh! No, no, I'm not complaining. I'm only trying to find the reasons why certain people are obliged to beg while others are short of nothing.'

'Well, if you go on trying to find these reasons, you'll go crackers, you'll go stark-staring bonkers; you just have to look at your hand: are your five fingers all equal? Nguirane, we're getting tired of your chatter!'

Nguirane picks up his guitar again, adjusts his glasses and asks everyone to join in his song:

> Salla, cook the couscous,
> A good *baasi salté*
> Cassava, beans and pumpkin,
> *Baasi salté Cayor*
> *Baasi salté Jolof*
> Richly dripping with buttery sauces
> Red with tomatoes
> *Baasi salté* fit for a king.

Chapter Ten

The whole night following the departure of the mysterious Kifi Bokoul, Mour could not sleep a wink. Nothing was easier than to buy a bull with a coat of one even colour, three times seven yards of a non-silky material, and seven hundred colas, but how is he to be able to distribute them around the City, when there aren't any beggars about any more? 'You must make your offerings exactly as indicated, otherwise things may go wrong—' What did Kifi Bokoul mean by that?— 'Isn't it possible to distribute the meat from house to house in the poor districts, as is usually done?'

Mour is well aware that in the poor districts there are people who would welcome with great joy meat like this, that they haven't the means to buy in the market. 'But', he reminds himself, 'Kifi Bokoul gave me very precise instructions; he said if I didn't respect them and things went wrong, it would be my own fault. A week later ... Where shall I find *bàttu*-bearers? ... What am I to do?'

Mour spent an anxious night reviewing all the means by which he might solve the problem: transport the meat out of the City, to another regional capital? – 'No, no, no, Kifi Bokoul specifically referred to the town where I live; no, that can't be possible ... What irony of fate! The beggars whose very existence I had forgotten for some time ... One never knows ... one never knows what the next day will bring ... Sally says they have a house, perhaps it would come to the same thing if I took the meat to them since they are the ones who used to walk about the streets begging ...'

Just as Mour was regretting that Kifi Bokoul was already far away, his thoughts wandered to Serigne Birama. He decided to go and consult Serigne Birama to find out if there were any ways of getting round the difficulty.

Mour started out before dawn, in order to be back for an important meeting at the Ministry, so the village of

Keur Gallo had hardly awoken from its slumbers when the large Mercedes drew up in front of Serigne Birama's house. Mour found Serigne Birama at prayer and had to wait for half an hour till the circle of beads had slipped through the bony fingers of the servant of the Lord. At one moment he had the impression as he watched the passion with which Serigne Birama abandoned his whole being to invocations and praises, that his revered marabout was in the process of losing his material presence and was about to take flight into the holy spheres of the spiritual world. He felt a deep emotion which only reinforced his faith in the man.

'Mour, Ndiaye, Ndiaye, Ndiaye. Are you in good health?'

'Sidibe, Serigne: Sidibe. I am in good health, Sidibe.'

'*Al hamdulilai*. We give thanks to God, Ndiaye. It has been a long time, quite a long time ... It is your work that detains you?'

'Yes, Serigne, it is only the work that has kept me; we are submerged. But even if I do not come, I never stop thinking of you for one moment.'

'I can believe you, Ndiaye. I know how it is, Ndiaye. Your body is not often here, but your hand is perpetually stretched out to us. God will repay you.'

'Amen, Sidibe ... Today I have a very important question to put to you, and you are the only person who can reassure me. This is how it is. I have to make a sacrifice ... the sacrifice of a bull ...'

'That is good. It is always good to make a sacrifice. It is a way of thanking the Creator who has entrusted to you what you offer to the poor to help them support their misery. It is good, every time you can, you must give. Fortune has no fixed domicile, God has not bestowed it for all time. He has only offered it on loan. One must never cease to remember that.'

'That is true, Sidibe ... That is true. But I am in a very difficult position ... In the City there are no more beggars in the streets; and it so happens that the sacrifice that I must make, must go to the beggars in the streets ... to the *boroom bàttu*, the begging-bowl-bearers.'

'How can that be? A city without beggars? ... But it is true that one day you told me that you were waging war on the beggars!'

'Yes, it was decided to get rid of them for reasons of development.'

Serigne lowered his head for a moment, in an attitude of meditation, then he raised it again, looked at Mour with a smile and said, 'You waged war against the beggars ... Who won?'

Mour was very embarrassed. He had been forced to admit that the distressing insecurity that he had felt ever since hearing Kifi Bokoul's verdict proved that the balance of power had been reversed. He believes firmly in the words of 'this man who is not human' and he is convinced that from this moment his whole fate is in the hands of the beggars whom he had driven away from their vantage points. But, it happens that he has set his mind on this post of Vice-President; he has placed all his hopes on it; he has even donned the mantle already, since his slightest action, his every plan, each one of his decisions is now thought out and executed in relation to his future – which is now imminent: 'in a week's time' – to his future situation as Vice-President of the Republic.

'*Chei yalla!* Eh, by Allah!' Serigne Birama continued. 'Everything is upside down in the world today!'

Mour tried, somewhat clumsily, to overcome his confusion and bring back a note of everyday humour to the discussion. Forcing a laugh he said, 'Hey, Serigne, you too! You don't like changes; but they're necessary, because the world is changing. And it changes more often for the good than for the bad. Just think. Before, it used to take months to get to the Holy Places. Now you can get there in a few hours.'

'That is true, but that is the work of the Lord ... Now, tell me, since you have driven the beggars away, why don't you give your donations in some other way? There are surely people in their own homes who are in need ...'

'In any case the beggars – those who haven't gone off to other regions – are still in the City; they have their house there. But ... the marabout who recommended me to make this sacrifice told me that I had to distribute it among the *bàttu*-bearers in the street, in all parts of the City. That's why I've come to ask you if I can take the sacrifice to the beggars' house ... You know, you are the only one who understands these things!'

'All right, all right! You must respect the instructions of your marabout.'

Mour thought he detected some caustic note in Serigne Birama's voice. He is very distressed.

'Oh, Serigne Birama, what are you saying? *You* are my marabout. You know you are the only one that I have an almost religious respect for; I place all my confidence in you; only certain others visit us at home ...'

'That's true. That's all right. There's no harm done. Do what he told you to do.'

After uttering these words, Serigne Birama took up his beads again. Mour did not dare interrupt him again. He took his leave and Serigne Birama replied to his greeting with a nod of his head.

In going to visit Serigne Birama, Mour had not had any lurking doubts for one moment that the holy man might not appreciate his need to consult other marabouts. But in the course of his journey back, as he was haunted with a thousand contradictory ideas, he decided that this was the explanation for Serigne Birama's attitude, and he suddenly had a feeling of guilt.

'No, I did not betray him! Not for anything in the world would I show ingratitude to Serigne Birama ... But can he be reproached for taking umbrage? ... I was lacking in tact, I oughtn't to have told him that I was seeing other marabouts ... It's as if I wanted to let him know that I don't think his prayers efficacious ... But then, it's only human to want to try everything to assure my chances . .. Serigne Birama is undoubtedly a man of great knowledge, but marabouts have different ways of reaching the realms of mystery, and Kifi Bokoul is said never to be wrong ... "A week later" ... But how shall I manage to respect his instructions to the letter?'

Mour turned up at his meeting an hour late, a thing

which had practically never happened with him before. His Minister-in-Charge looked at his watch very pointedly when Mour made his appearance in the large committee-room, and glanced at him contemptuously. Mour apologised to the 'ladies and gentlemen present', with the excuse that he had had an appointment with his doctor who had kept him longer than he had anticipated, then, as Keba smiled at him deferentially, he smiled back. He listened to the Minister with half an ear as he spoke of the necessity to clear the last 'insanitary zones' from the residential areas. Then, in a weary voice, and with his eyes glued to the document in front of him, he drew attention to the difficulty of the project: 'The slightest mistake may result in failure; after all these people own their property and won't understand that we wish to expropriate them, because they're poor and can't rebuild; that's the root of the problem: however much we compensate them, they are bound to underestimate the amount granted them, and will think themselves hard done by ... So we shall have to set up a very shrewd strategy before we confront them ... We shall have to act with tact and diplomacy ...'

The Minister interrupted him with an ironic smile: 'Monsieur Ndiaye, it's not a question of diplomacy, really! ... but of using our brains. You must know how to use your brains in order to succeed ... there are matters in which diplomacy doesn't work and, believe me, all the delicate problems of the beggars to which Monsieur Keba Dabo found a brilliant solution ... all these serious problems ... do you think that diplomacy would have sufficed to resolve them! ... No, certainly not! You must tackle them in a scientific manner: evaluate the various approaches and the ways of intervening.'

Mour did not think it would serve any purpose to reply to the Minister's domineering retort; he simply looked at him with the same amused glance that the cook reserves for the chicken while it's still alive, with the certainty that one day, in the very near future, it will be on the grill.

The Minister went on, 'Consequently, I give you ten days to present me with as complete a report as possible on the ways and means of clearing the insanitary zones of the City.'

And turning to Keba Dabo, he added, 'Monsieur Dabo, we have complete confidence in you!'

Chapter Eleven

Mour has spent three long sleepless nights, three wretched nights of unanswered questions, nights of anguish during which he has been constantly assailed by distress at having caused pain to Serigne Birama, combined with his unshaken and increasingly imperative yearning to achieve his ambition, and finally the agony caused by his inability to carry out the sacrifice.

In his mind's eye he saw the blurred image of the Holy Scriptures with their yellowing pages, heaped up on the mats and occupying the whole length of Serigne Birama's rectangular hut ... 'The fine white ram which I sent him will probably put me back in his good books ... He will only know how much he means to me when I am appointed, *Insh' Allah* ... A week after the sacrifice ...'

Then the image of Kifi Bokoul loomed up again before him: the voluminous chechia, the blue boubou, the two bottomless apertures in what it was agreed to call his face ... 'in what our human logic persuades us to take for a face ... for this creature is not a man ... What are his hands, his feet, his nose like ...?'

In a state of semi-hallucination, he saw *bàttu* clashing under his nose, held out by beggars in rags and tatters and looking physical wrecks. He came down to earth again, decided to settle the whole business, at the same time ensuring that his wishes would be fulfilled. He would not accept failure.

'This offering ... I shall make it in the prescribed manner ... whatever it may cost me ... I shall have this post of Vice-President ... I must have it.'

Deciding to settle the matter, he got up earlier than usual; he pointed towards the four points of the compass with the magic horn filled with cowries, that Kifi Bokoul had given him, waited on his prayer-mat for the sun to rise, then ventured out on a drive through the City in the hope of meeting, in the early hours of the morning, a few diehards among the beggars whose greed for easy earnings was stronger than their fear of being hunted down and clobbered ... Not a soul! Not a single solitary soul! He drove through every part of the City, the beggars' vantage points were deserted, hopelessly deserted! Anger, rage ... against whom? Mour has no idea. He feels a prickling sensation in his stomach ... Hunger? Perhaps ... But hunger can wait ... wait until ambition, that is growing by the hour, is satisfied.

'No!' He did not return home to have breakfast. He went to his office and threw himself exhausted into an armchair – not the one at his desk – but one of the armchairs that are arranged in one corner of his office like a little sitting-room. He dropped his brief-case on the carpet. A few minutes later Keba came in, a note-book and a pen in his hands.

'Good-morning, sir.'

'Good-morning Keba.'

Keba hesitated: should he sit at the desk or ...

'Come and sit here, Keba.'

Mour indicated an armchair opposite the one he had flopped down into, with his legs apart, his feet under the coffee-table, his hands clasped on his belly. Keba noticed the black rings round his chief's eyes but did not try to find out the explanation.

'I sent for you ... It's about the beggars again ...'

Keba did not understand, he even felt somewhat disconcerted. To talk to him about beggars again, so early in the morning, when he had practically forgotten their existence, when he had felt liberated from the burden they had caused him! He did not understand, and he preferred to let Mour explain.

'Where are they now?'

'I really couldn't tell you, sir. Since we have achieved our objective, since no one risks meeting a beggar anywhere, I have not worried myself about the spot where they might have gone to earth. Perhaps they have simply returned to their villages.'

Mour once again discerned Keba's youthful exuberance and enthusiasm in his gestures and in his whole being. He had been hesitant to carry out his intentions to the bitter end, but he was immediately reassured by the total loyalty that Keba had always shown him. And besides he felt at the end of his tether, really at the end of his tether.

'No, they haven't gone back to their villages. They are on the outskirts of the City, in the new Slum-Clearance Resettlement Area ... In any case, they never go out, they stay permanently indoors.'

'The main thing is that they don't overrun the City any more.'

'Yes ... yes. But Keba, I must tell you ... I need these beggars today. I need them ... I've got to distribute a sacrifice among them. I need them to go back to their vantage points for one day, for one day only ... It won't even be for one day, only for a few hours!'

Keba, completely nonplussed, slightly loosened his tie to give himself time to think; he felt himself growing hot all over and his head began to swim. He had difficulty in getting his breath. In a timid, almost inaudible voice, he asked Mour, 'You want the beggars back in the City? ... Is that what you're saying?'

'Yes, for a very personal reason ... I'd like you to go to see them with a few members of the former clearance squads to give them confidence and to persuade them to come back on the streets for a few hours. Tell them they risk nothing, absolutely nothing!'

Keba did not reply immediately. He lowered his eyes to his note-book for a few minutes during which Mour watched the vein which stood out on the forehead of his faithful assistant, and said to himself that Keba was certainly trying to find a solution, a way of dealing with the beggars. Finally Keba raised his head, and prompted by some violent emotion stared at his chief and cried passionately, 'No! Who do you take me for! It's madness what you're saying! I've hunted down these beggars, I've destroyed them physically and morally, and finally they leave us in peace, and now you want me to go and tell them to come back! What would I look like? Now that we can finally breathe freely, you want me to pollute the atmosphere again! You ask me to open a sore that has not yet healed. No! Not on your life! I won't do it!'

He stood up, facing Mour. The latter tried to catch him by the arm to calm him down, but he didn't succeed. Then he raised his voice threateningly.

'Keba, that's enough! That's enough, I say! Don't forget I'm your superior and I won't allow you to be disrespectful to me, under any pretext!'

'Do what you like! Have me suspended or sacked even. I don't care! I don't care a damn!'

He turned towards the door. Mour jumped up hurriedly to catch him. He was in a pitiful state, was Mour! A man you would have thought incapable of weakness. Keba is acting as much from anger and contempt, as from pain at seeing a man fall so low, to descend to such depths for reasons that so far he cannot explain.

'Wait, Keba ... I've always considered you as one of my own family, not just as an assistant ... God alone knows the admiration I feel for you!'

He has finally succeeded in making Keba sit down again.

'Listen Keba ... It can happen to any of us to take certain steps that afterwards turn against us, without such an eventuality having ever occurred to us ... This problem of the beggars, we didn't think about it enough, perhaps we ought to have looked for another way of resolving it, a way which did not mean totally destroying all the bridges between them and us ... Don't worry, I'm not accusing you of not having done your job properly, on the contrary, since I answered for it one hundred per cent, and I'm not in the habit of making spectacular U-turns ... Only, you see, we have certain beliefs that we can't throw overboard overnight, it needs time to prepare the ground ...'

As he speaks Mour has almost succeeded in regaining his self-possession, whereas Keba systematically refuses to look him in the face; he lets his gaze wander around the office over the armchairs, the table, the ceiling, the photograph of the President, the wall-to-wall carpet and the pictures by famous artists.

'If I'm reduced to asking you to do what I've just asked you to do,' Mour went on, 'do you think I'm just acting out of caprice? We are men, Keba; if a man found himself today in a critical situation, faced with an insoluble crisis, and he had been instructed to make an offering as the only means of salvation, what do you think he would do? Just imagine the anguish of this man who had been brought up from his most tender childhood to believe that he could gain relief from all his fears, all his apprehensions, all his nightmares, his dreads, by giving three lumps of sugar, a candle, a length of material, in a word all kinds of objects to beggars! Can one chuck all these beliefs overboard in one night?'

Keba has not opened his mouth once. Besides, what is there for him to say? When *he* was young, he was one of the people who were the recipients of charity; he never had the opportunity of gaining relief from any anguish by giving to charity. He had had to live with his torments, his misery, his suffering; his mother lived with them; his brothers lived with them; they suffered them till they were forgotten. So he can't reason like those who find relief in giving: he has never known any other consolation than that brought by time.

When he passed nervously through his secretary's office on the way back to his own desk, Sagar Diouf had a shrewd idea that something had happened; she noted his nervous state, she saw his blood-shot eyes and the vein throbbing in his temple. She thought of a thousand possibilities before she made up her mind to go and ask him what was the matter.

'It's just that there are certain things that I simply can't accept! No, I won't tolerate being used as a servant or an errand boy. I'm a Government servant and I serve the Government and not one man.'

'But you know very well, Keba, that everyone realises you're not anyone's servant!'

'No, that's just it, Monsieur Ndiaye doesn't realise it. He's just asked me, for personal reasons – you hear that! for personal reasons! – to go and dig out the beggars, goodness knows where, so that he can give them goodness knows what! The Government's decision about cleaning up the City doesn't count any more; Monsieur Ndiaye's wishes must come first. No, no and no!'

'If I were you, I'd adopt a different attitude, rather than opposing him with a categorical refusal.'

'What attitude?'

'You know, Keba, you're not always very easy to get on with ... Nevertheless, it's time you began to open your eyes a bit ... Do you want me to tell you what I think?'

'Go on.'

'Well, Keba, it's like this; you can't live divorced from your own times and the society you belong to. It's not for nothing that people say that when you're in Rome you must do as Rome does ... You must follow the rhythm of the dance and if everyone dances on one foot, so must you ... Isn't that true, Keba?'

'Well ... it all depends! ... It depends on where the dance is being organised. If we risk falling down a precipice by dancing on one foot, I prefer to remain on my two feet. It's safer and it's more comfortable in any case!'

Sagar Diouf laughed and succeeded in stimulating Keba to a little smile, which encouraged her to go on.

'I'm quite sure that what Monsieur Ndiaye asks you to do has got something to do with the eventual appointment of a Vice-President. Everyone's saying that he'll be Vice-President and I believe he will. So, it would be better to keep on good terms with him ... all the more so, so as he won't forget you when he's appointed. At the stage he's reached, he's got heaps of offerings to make; you see now that what I said to you about the beggars is true! ... So, since he wants to see the beggars and you're the only one who can help him to do so, why don't you make the most of the opportunity?'

'What opportunity?'

'Well, if I were in your shoes, I'd cash in on it. He's got a lot at stake; he wouldn't hesitate to do anything you asked for. That's life; one must know how to take advantage of a situation, and you wouldn't be doing any harm. Look how rich he's got, while you're the one who's always done the work ... Without even giving the impression that you want him to pay for the service he's asking you, tell him that you'd like to get a bigger house and that you need his help.'

The look that Keba gave Sagar Diouf betrayed enormous disappointment and profound indignation. Without giving way to the anger that might have been expected from him in similar circumstances, Keba said in a voice almost devoid of any expression, 'I'll never be a party to such sordid, odious bargains, which are contrary to human dignity ... You can go back to your office.'

Chapter Twelve

In the City, only one subject of conversation, only one thing on everyone's mind: 'The cabinet reshuffle and the appointment of a Vice-President are imminent, and the competition will be close!'

For some time Raabi has been studying her father's slightest actions, his slightest reactions; she has noticed that he is at home more regularly than usual; he shuts himself up for whole nights – even those which he would normally have spent with his second wife – in a room set aside for prayers, furnished only with oriental carpets and from which an intoxicating smell of incense is given off. Since Mour married Sine, Raabi has been unable to make up her mind to adopt the necessary objectivity or even a certain diplomacy which would help her to hide her resentment. She disapproves of pretence and hypocrisy; that is why she has never been moved by her father's many attempts to ingratiate himself, his generous actions, his repeated, poignant demonstrations of affection which is not returned. She has never responded to Lolli's repeated attempts to reason with her: 'Raabi, everything wears off. One must learn to forget. And after all, you mustn't lose sight of the fact that your father is your father and you have no right to judge him; that can bring you misfortune.'

Raabi never told her mother her true feelings; every time she listened to her with a smile, giving her the impression that she didn't attach any importance to what she did in fact consider a serious situation.

One day, however, noticing her father's extreme lassitude, she asked Lolli, 'Why is my father so agitated? Is it because of the public rumour that is talking about him as if he were already the Vice-President of the Republic?'

'He's been the victim of a nasty trick of fate. But it's a good thing. These tricks of fate are sent by the Creator to try his servants, to test their loyalty and their belief ...

Afterwards, good fortune will follow.'

'What's happened to him?'

Lolli told her daughter the whole story of the beggars, which she already knew from having read about it in the newspapers, heard it on the radio, seen it on television; she also told her about the sacrifice which had been prescribed and Keba's disloyalty; 'a man Mour had done everything for and who would never have had such a fine position – a good salary, a car, a secretary – without Mour's foresight'. From everything that Lolli told her daughter, Lolli has drawn the conclusion that people are jealous and that it is more necessary than ever not to trust anyone, not even 'one's own shadow'.

'But your father is too good; he never thinks badly of anyone; he has a heart of gold and that will probably be his salvation!'

Lolli had scarcely finished speaking when Mour burst into the room. Raabi got up abruptly from the bed where she had been sitting beside her mother, and made for the door, just avoiding her father who did not pay any attention to her and did not even hear her say 'Good morning, father'. When she had gone a little way towards the sitting-room, she heard Lolli calling, 'Sally, Sally!'

Chapter Thirteen

'Is it much further?' Mour asked, seething with impatience.

'When the tarred road gives out', the chauffeur replied, 'there is a long sandy track that we must follow for about five miles before reaching the new Slum-Clearance Resettlement Area.'

As soon as the tarred road was out of sight Mour had the impression that the car was lost in a wilderness which seemed to stretch to infinity: a dreary, bare landscape, lifeless, swept by a wind of such violence that its howls mingled with the clouds of dust whipped up from the sand-dunes and with the fierce moans of the sea that foamed in fury.

Mour has never set foot in these parts, he only knew of their existence from maps on which they are marked in red; that indicated vacant zones in which a good part of the population could be accommodated. He is also discovering other realities, without even being aware of it: neither the skilful manoeuvres of his chauffeur, nor the swaying of the car from side to side, nor the murky atmosphere that he tries to penetrate from behind his dark glasses, can hold his attention; what intrigues him is that he has not yet glimpsed any houses.

'Sally, are you sure this is the right place? You haven't made a mistake?'

Sally turns round slightly towards the back seat. 'We'll soon be there, sir.'

The chauffeur confirms this. 'This is the right place. Those buses we're passing are all coming from there …'

Mour is reassured and can once more follow the drift of his own thoughts. Seated in the right corner of the back seat of the car, dressed in a simple boubou and slippers, to put the beggars at ease, he cannot imagine that his errand can fail. 'I'll pay whatever is necessary.'

'One week later … Is it fitting that such a simple thing

as a shortage of beggars should make me miss the part in the national destiny that I am called upon to play? A bull, twenty-one yards of material, seven hundred cola-nuts, that's enough to make an unforgettable feast ... Since they've taken refuge in this wilderness, the paupers must be hungry ... No, they will never have seen so much munificence in one day ...'

The chauffeur parked the car in front of a house surrounded by a green-painted fence, and turned to his employer, 'We're here, sir. This is the beggars' house.'

'Oh! So you knew it ...'

'Yes, yes, sir. Everyone knows this place, sir!'

'Assalamu alleikum!'

'Malikum salam.'

No one has moved, nobody is interested in knowing the identity of the visitor who has just parked such a large car in front of the house. They are used now to this type of visit. Nguirane Sarr, in his suit and tie, continues to draw plaintive melodies from his guitar; he sings the song of friendship that a little girl composed in far-off times to immortalise her play-mate, the hippopotamus, who was shot by a cruel hunter.

Salla Niang is seated on her mat playing with some cowrie-shells; her head-scarf is tied in a peak on top of her head, her legs stretched out and crossed in front of her, and a long tooth-pick is stuck in the corner of her mouth. And then there is this crowd of beggars moving about, chatting, or lying asleep or scratching themselves amidst the continual squalling of the babies who are playing in the sand in the courtyard.

Mour is struck by the sight. Astonishment rather than compassion. He has never seen, as if simultaneously projected onto a screen, the image of so many physical defects, so much physical decrepitude and human disintegration from which, it is true, some patches of light stand out, like this Salla Niang whose face gleams like a bronze bust, fashioned by a master sculptor. By spontaneous association of ideas he begins to think of certain insalubrious districts of the City, certain slums in the middle of which stand a few buildings in ostentatiously luxurious style, like castles standing in solitary state.

'*Mba jamm ngeen am?* Are you in peace?'

'*Tabarak Allah!* We give thanks to God!'

'Who is the master of this house?'

Only now does Salla Niang raise her eyes to look at the visitor.

'What do you want?'

'I'd like to speak to the master of the house.'

'I'm in charge here.'

A clarion-call of a voice, clear and crystalline like a stream of molten silver. Mour is silent for a moment, then begins to wonder what kind of links there might be between this lady and these beggars.

'I've come about a matter concerning the beggars ...'

'Ah ...'

Mour would have felt more at ease if he had been invited to sit down, but Salla makes no move in this direction. She asks Nguirane to approach and the others to listen to 'the visitor who wishes to speak to us'.

Since his arrival Mour has noticed frequent comings and goings: he has seen people making donations to the first beggar they meet; he has seen others going the rounds of the *bàttu*-bearers, examining them closely without being in the least shocked, and finally making their gift to the chosen one. He thinks to himself that these people are possibly not as wretched as one might have imagined. 'But then, how do they make use of everything they receive? Why don't certain ones of them aspire to more cleanliness, more decency? Could they possibly have taken on the identity of the mask that they had been obliged to wear in order to arouse people's pity, to such a point that now that their situation is visibly improved, they continue to play the game of poverty and starvation?'

'This is the reason for my visit to these parts: I have a very, very important sacrifice to make. You are the ones I am going to offer it to, but I cannot bring it to you here. It is essential that tomorrow morning – tomorrow morning only – it will only be for a few hours – it is essential that tomorrow you go to take up your regular vantage points. You must take up your stands in every part of the City! Just as you used to do before; in front of the markets, at the entrance to the hospitals, at the traffic-lights, in front of offices, clinics, banks, shops, throughout the City, in every part of the City. You will receive offerings from me, offerings that will make it worth your while having taken the trouble to travel from here. And besides, you've been huddled together here for such a long time, as if you were scarcely human. For once in a while get out and about, at least to stretch your legs a bit!'

If it had not been for the laughter that greeted him from every side, Mour would have continued his speech; he had been trapped, without realising it, by the demon of eloquence by which he stirred up and magnetised the crowds in political arenas.

'Go out into the streets, can you be serious?'

'Now that we are here in peace, to expose ourselves to harassment again!'

'Such an action would be to return voluntarily to a hell from which the Lord has delivered us!'

'May the Lord preserve us from that! May he preserve us! *Yalla Tere!* May the Lord preserve us!'

'You don't risk anything, absolutely nothing! I guarantee that nothing will happen to you. It will simply be a matter of going to get what I shall be giving you, and you won't regret it!'

Mour has deliberately tried to arouse the greed of certain of the beggars, but he does not seem to have succeeded.

'Besides,' says Nguirane Sarr, 'who are you, to talk to us like this and guarantee our safety?'

'I am the Director of the Public Health Service. I am in charge of all the people who might cause you any trouble.'

'Ah! ... So you are Mour Ndiaye, who they talk about on the radio every day?'

Mour's heart swelled with pride as he replied to Nguirane, 'Yes, that's me. You have nothing to fear.'

The news is immediately shouted throughout the

gathering: 'It's Mour Ndiaye!'; 'Mour Ndiaye has come to talk to us'; '*Ngoor si nyeu*, the gentleman who's here, Mour Ndiaye, here ...'

Salla has not yet opened her mouth. She has simply watched the scene. Nguirane Sarr has got up, placed his guitar on the chair that he had been sitting on, straightened his jacket and tie and says in a voice that seemed to Mour mocking and disrespectful,

'So, governor, you drove us away and now you're the one who comes to fetch us back! What may be the reason for this, if I may ask?'

Salla smiles in complicity.

Mour is astonished at the impertinence of this beggar; he could never have imagined that so much effrontery in voice and manner could be found in a blind man who depends on others for his existence. 'So they start cheeking us now!' Mour almost gives way to the temptation to put this fellow in his place, but he speedily remembers that he is obliged to contain his irritation and to try to establish a peaceful dialogue with these people. Haunted by the idea of failure and bedevilled by the obsession of the sacrifice – 'a week later, the Vice-Presidency' – he deliberately chooses to play his last card, that of dishonesty.

'We don't have to misunderstand each other, chaps. Have you ever seen me intervening directly, in person, in the war waged against you?'

General silence.

'We bosses, we're in an awkward position; we're made responsible for everything, and God only knows that we haven't the slightest idea of half the actions that our inspectors commit; they do as they like and then people say that it's the chief.'

Mour realises that his attempts to justify himself have fallen flat, so he changes his tactics. 'You've got radio sets, haven't you? You listen to the radio every day, so you must have heard all last week programmes broadcasting information to citizens and particularly those who are eligible for pensions ... You've heard what's happened, haven't you?'

No one replied to Mour's questions. He tries to detect some reaction in the silent crowd; then he turns to Salla Niang and Nguirane Sarr, but neither of them seems to have heard what he has just said. He continues: 'You know that some contemptible individuals were depriving widows of their just dues, which is contrary to our religion and to what is right. In order to get someone to see to their papers, these poor women were paying considerable sums in advance to government inspectors, who are paid by the Government to do this work. Do you think that their chiefs knew what was going on? – Certainly not, since they were severely punished as soon as the administration became aware of the inhuman transactions that they were involved in. Can you imagine that these widows, who hadn't the means to pay in advance, were being put in touch with 'money-lenders' who advanced them the sums demanded with huge interest and against papers that they had to sign, to prove that they owed money! And then after making hundreds of applications, going from one office to another, going backwards and forwards in vain, and receiving hundreds of promises, these poor widows finally reached the right department to find themselves faced with creditors who sometimes took their whole pension. All that is the fault of unscrupulous employees, acting contrary to their superiors' directives ... You can see that this business is far more serious than yours ... yes, more serious, in as much as you, at least, you are here and you manage to find enough to live on. But a widow, a woman all alone, who often has no work, who has no support, with her whole family! Their sufferings only ceased on the day that the heads of departments realised what had been going on.'

The heavy silence which greets Mour's flight of oratory deeply disappoints him. His story has neither convinced nor moved the beggars. So, then, Mour decides to put his cards on the table.

'Can I count on you tomorrow? I'm prepared to satisfy all your demands!'

Thereupon he hears on all sides a murmur which gives him a little hope. He looks again at Nguirane Sarr who has already resumed his seat and placed his guitar on his lap. Mour decides to address him familiarly. 'You fellow with the guitar, what do you say?'

'You're asking us to return to the same places that you yourself drove us away from!'

Mour is worried. Very worried. On the brink of despair. But he must not give in, he must win the battle ... 'One week later ... And they are there, in front of me, on them my destiny depends ... But this blind beggar, what pig-headedness! ... God is the Creator of all things, He alone knows why he has ordered the world as He has done ... For if this blind man had his sight, he would have been a phenomenon!'

'Guitar-player, you have not understood what I have just said to you! It is my men who went too far!'

'They weren't satisfied with driving us away, they tracked us down, flogged us, beat us like dogs!

'They are men who act without thought; they are inhuman! I have never been informed of this savage behaviour! Go back on the streets tomorrow, and you'll see if they lay a hand on you!'

'You drove us away!'

Now Salla Niang finds the scene amusing. Mour's appearance of being out-manoeuvred, Nguirane's grave countenance. The crowd's indifference. She bursts into peals of laughter: 'What a liar, what a damned liar! ... If my former employer's countless marabouts had challenged him when he was waging such a heated campaign against marabouts, he'd have denied that he was the main person responsible for the anti-marabout campaign ... But why do they wear a reversible boubou! Why don't they remain what they are, and show their real face! ... *Nii noo seu!* How petty they are! They'll go anywhere to follow their ambition or if it's in their own interests, even if they go to the devil.'

She has made up her mind to get rid of Mour. He is visibly at the end of his tether. She is pitiless; her humour turns to derision; the sight of him irritates her.

'Monsieur Ndiaye, you can go. Tomorrow, if it please the Creator, all the beggars will be back at their old posts.'

Mour feels an enormous weight lifted from his chest. He can finally breathe again!

'They will be back at their posts?'

'Certainly', Salla replied, 'they will go ...'

'Thank you, sister. You see, we are all equal, we are all of the same condition, for we are all human; so we should find grounds for agreement on every occasion. Thank you, sister.'

When he has once more passed through the gate of the property, Salla hastens to say to her fellow-beggars, 'Don't budge from here. No one is to budge from here ever again! Tomorrow, we shall see that he bites the dust!'

Nguirane Sarr is seized with uncontrollable laughter, so uncontrollable and so infectious that all the beggars join in the general hilarity. When everyone has rejoiced at what they call Mour's 'madness' – 'it's because he's mad that he dared to come here to seek us out' – Nguirane Sarr, acting the buffoon this time, imitates blows being most energetically administered, saying, 'Salla, you have the knack of plying the whip without even raising your little finger. Swi-i-sh-sh! Swi-i-sh-sh! Swi-i-sh-sh! Poor fellow, he'll be none the worse for it – just a bruised back. Nothing serious.'

Chapter Fourteen

Mour purchased the best bull that he could find at the cattle market and paid a fortune for it. When he expressed his preferences as to the colour of the coat, the experienced dealers took the hint, immediately guessing the destination of the bull, and speculated on how much it meant to him, but Mour did not in the least think he had been done, for he would have paid any price for his fawn bull.

The next day, before the first prayers at day-break, the two expert butchers whom he had summoned slaughtered the beast, and before you could say Jack Robinson, they had cut it up and filled two huge basins with good fat meat. Early as it was, Raabi watched the whole scene from her window, less attracted by the slaughter of the bull – it was a sight to which the household had become familiar for some years – than by her father's zeal, for it was the first time that she had seen him participating directly in the operations. Mour ran hither and thither till he was completely breathless, lifted huge quarters of meat and cut them into smaller portions. Then he took a large piece of oilcloth, spread it on the ground and laid out eleven rows, each of seven heaps of meat; he wouldn't let anyone help him in this task of dividing up the portions. 'No, leave me alone, otherwise I'll get mixed up.' Raabi watched him counting the number of heaps over and over again with an air of devotion, and as she watched and saw his white clothes all stained with blood, as she watched him stooping down, wrapping up the seventy-seven heaps of meat in seventy-seven cellophane bags, walking backwards and forwards carrying them clumsily all by himself and placing them carefully in huge bowls, she tried to find an explanation for so much zeal, but could find none, not having been informed of the period of one week that Kifi Bokoul had set for Mour, for if Mour had told Lolli of his conversation with Kifi Bokoul, he had deliberately omitted any mention of the period set for the realisation of his ambitions: it was too good to be true, too close, so that out of superstition he was afraid to say a word about it.

Mour loaded the seventy-seven packets of meat, the seven hundred cola-nuts and the three times seven yards of non-silky white material into a van. With a light heart he took his seat beside the driver, having allocated to himself the role of distributing the parcels as they met the beggars. 'All I shall have to do is to lift a packet out of the bowls and in that way Kouli won't have to stop for long … just to slow down a little …'

Not a soul in his own neighbourhood; no one in front of the baker's, no one in front of the chemist's, not a beggar in front of the grocer's. Mour is somewhat put out; he certainly could have wished that the beggars would have thought of coming as far as this, on this particular morning, but he knows that they have never particularly frequented this neighbourhood.

'Kouli, drive on towards the Main Market!'

Previously, the Main Market constituted the beggars' rallying ground when they were driven out from their various vantage points in the centre of the City.

Not a soul at the Main Market; no *talibés*, no beggars, no *bàttu*. Mour's heart begins to beat faster. He refuses to give up hope, he remembers the assured tone in which 'the lady with the beggars' had told him they would go back to their places in the streets. 'No, she can't have been lying to me, no.'

'Kouli, let's go on a bit further towards the main streets, where there are a lot of crossings with traffic-lights, then you must go to the mosques, as it's Friday today perhaps there are some who have gone to take up their position in front of the mosques.'

At the traffic-lights, in front of the mosques, no beggars, no *talibés*, no *bàttu*. Then Mour feels a weight on his chest, he has difficulty in breathing, there is a ringing in his ears.

'Let's drive round the town once more. They live a long

way out, perhaps they haven't been able to find transport so early …'

'Possibly', Kouli replies, 'where they live it's quite a problem to get a bus early in the morning. When you do see one six or seven hundred yards away, there's a whole crowd of people waiting already at the bus-stop and they rush at it and it's soon full up. So only the able-bodied men get on first. Beggars and women aren't strong enough to face the scuffle which often degenerates into a free-for-all.'

Kouli's words are like balm to Mour's heart.

'Yes, that must be the reason! No buses! … Oh, yes, that's another problem … The vast mass of workers live in those outlying districts.'

'Some of them have to get up at half past four to get to work in time …'

'Kouli, drive round by the central hospital!'

At the central hospital, no beggars, no *talibés*. They scour the whole City; not a *bàttu* in sight.

The golden globe of the sun has dispersed the morning mist in which the atmosphere was veiled and now its burning arrows are radiated throughout the City, dazzling Kouli when he turns in certain directions.

Mour can no longer be in any doubt when, at his request, Kouli parks the lorry for two whole hours at the Main Market, in front of the bus-stop which served the neighbourhood where the beggars live. Not a single beggar alights from the buses.

Mour is absolutely shattered, while at the same time he is overcome with fury. 'The rogues! the hypocrites! the liars! That's the reason why they are reduced to begging … They've only got what they deserve!'

What can he do with seventy-seven cellophane bags full of meat, seven hundred cola-nuts, three times seven yards of white, non-silky material? … 'They've taken me for a ride, they've deliberately deceived me! … That woman lied to me shamelessly! … They'll pay for it one day … I'll get even with that rabble yet! Just let them wait!'

What is he to do? For the moment they've got the power in their hands …

'Kouli, let's go to the place where they live!'

The bustle of the Main Market; clusters of humanity swarming in all directions; an interminable din; dealers calling out; shouts from the auction sales, arguments and insults exchanged between lookers-on and pedlars, but bursts of laughter here and there; the delicate tints of the fruit and vegetables piled up along the pavements; the brighter hues of multicoloured objects that fill the stalls; the kaleidoscopic effect of the majestic boubous worn by the men and women who stroll around the market.

Along the streets, the ceaseless procession of hurried workers, carefree schoolchildren, energetic housewives who hurry by – in spite of the weight of their shopping baskets – still careful not to jolt unnecessarily the baby tied on their backs and who still sleeps the sleep of the innocent.

The whole City is now flooded with a brilliant, scorching light. Kouli keeps his foot down on the accelerator and the tarmac rolls by at a breakneck speed and in the distance patches of light gleam, but these are nothing but mirages.

Mour sees nothing of all this. The sandy track … a wilderness which seems lacking in any oases or any boundaries. Mour's jangled nerves can hardly bear any more. Today he feels every jolt; the van is less smooth-running than the Mercedes; several times he has had to reach over to the back to stop the bags of meat from falling off.

The beggars' house. The whole brotherhood is there; the place is literally invaded: the morning's offerings are arriving. Out of discretion Mour asks Kouli to turn round and park a little way off, while they wait for the crowd to diminish.

'There's not even a tree here to give a bit of shade to wait in. You'll be very hot in the sun,' Kouli ventures anxiously.

'That's nothing. It isn't important.'

Inside the van it is like a furnace, in spite of the open windows. Kouli is upset by his employer's discomfort. He tries out all sorts of subjects of conversation that discretion permits: the heat that promises to be interminable; the distance of this neighbourhood which doesn't seem to discourage people; the way they overdo it, instead of offering their sacrifice and then going away, they stay an eternity worrying about things that don't even concern them.

Mour replies with the utmost brevity to all these attempts to engage him in conversation.

'Would you like me to go and get you something to drink from the Moor's shop, sir?'

'Yes, that's a good idea! Here, get me anything, coke, orangeade, anything.'

In a few moments Kouli is back.

'I've brought you a lemonade, but it's not ice-cold; he says that the ice hasn't arrived yet.'

'All right. That doesn't matter.'

It is almost noon when Mour enters the beggars' domain. He stares at Nguirane resentfully as the latter sits in a corner, near the entrance, plucking his guitar. He looks for Salla Niang and catches sight of her at the other end of the yard, in front of her stove. Finally he calls out a greeting to which comes a murmured, indistinct reply. He advances towards Salla, followed by Kouli. He tries to control his anger, but he cannot manage to stop his heart beating faster, a fact that Salla Niang is not slow to notice.

'Good-day, sister; are you in peace?'

'*Tabarakala*. I give thanks to God.'

Mour is struck – disagreeably struck – by Salla's very ostentatious air of indifference. She goes on stoking up her stove, without looking up, 'as if she was not the one who yesterday made me a firm promise which has not been respected! ... Not even any explanation, or ... does she perhaps expect me to ask her for one? There are some types of behaviour that it's very hard to swallow ... these people that I would never have come into contact with if it hadn't been for this sacrifice ... who are possibly the only ones in the whole town who dare to receive me with so little consideration. But today I am the one who needs them ... I shall have to put up with their behaviour ...'

Mour is standing like a stuffed dummy in front of Salla Niang who has taken the lid off her cook-pot and has put the onions into the hot oil, then adding a bowl of tomato paste diluted with water, she stirs and stirs the boiling sauce continuously; she doesn't seem to see Mour or the uniformed chauffeur standing a few yards behind his employer.

'I must put up with everything. Negotiate, discuss, to achieve my end ... The day when I get my own back ...'

'Sister, I came to see what had held the lads up ... They promised to be back at their old posts, in the City.'

After a few moments Salla deigns to look up at Mour. 'What held them up? I don't know. Ask them yourself. They aren't children and I'm not their mother.'

Mour is astonished at Salla's aggressive tone. He makes an effort not to show his feelings. In a conciliatory voice, a smile on his lips, he says to Salla, 'What you say is true. But if I thought right to confer with you, it is because you are the one I spoke with yesterday ... This morning, when I didn't see them, I realised I had not given them the money for their bus-fares; it was an omission on my part; it was completely my fault.'

Then turning round briskly without giving Salla the time to reply, Mour looked for the best place from which he could address the whole gathering and be heard by them all.

'My greetings to you, lads!'

Without waiting for a reply, and to take them by surprise, Mour dips his hand into the pocket of his boubou, bringing out wads of bank-notes which he hurls towards the beggars; the majority of the crowd immediately jump up to seize the notes as they flutter in the wind. They jostle each other shouting, 'Money's flying about! Money's flying about!'

'That's for your bus-fares; so you can go into town and take up your places in the streets, can't you?'

As if electrified, the crowd hops up and down, laughing and some even praise Mour's generosity.

'Yes, yes, we'll come!'

Even the blind beggars hurl themselves into the *mêlée*;

most of them haven't a chance with those who have full use of their eyes; a few, guided by some instinct, make an effort and catch some notes in the air. Mour, seeing the effect he has produced, penetrates into the thick of the scrimmage; the crowd falls on him now, swarming like bees all round him; arms are raised high giving the impression of an army of basket-ball players waiting excitedly for the ball which hangs above the net; Mour throws out more wads of notes.

'You will come, won't you?'

'Sure, we'll come. We'll come this afternoon!'

'The money's flying about, it's flying everywhere.'

'Come! you won't regret it; I guarantee you won't be sorry.'

It's raining bank-notes. Mour is pleased to see that Salla is in the midst of the scrum; that's a good sign, he thinks. To placate her and to make her better disposed towards him, Mour throws a whole wad in her direction so that she can easily catch a good share. She has lost her head-scarf in the scuffle. Mour interprets her broad smile as an undoubted victory for himself. He is jubilant. It is only now, he thinks, that he has managed to break down the wall that separated him from the beggars.

Kouli, dumbfounded, watches the scene in silence. What a waste of so much money! How can his employer be a party to this circus amidst all these beggars! Kouli doesn't take his eyes off Salla Niang; he hates her for her behaviour just now towards his employer. 'And yet she made a rush for the money!' Kouli is sorry for his employer, deeply sorry for him.

When calm has been restored, Mour once more addresses the gathering: 'Immediately after the *Tisbaar* prayer, I'll drive through the town to give you your alms. You will be there, won't you?'

'We'll be there. Oh, yes, we'll be there,' several voices call out.

As he reaches the gate again, Mour starts: he sees 'the cheeky blind beggar with the guitar' still sitting on his chair, with his guitar on his lap, motionless as a block of stone. Clearly he has never moved.

'So much the worse for him,' Mour thinks. 'The others will have filled their pockets.'

The van doesn't seem so uncomfortable now. His nervous excitement has given way to the lightness of heart that results from victory in a difficult fight.

'Other people give them everything,' he explains to Kouli, 'everything except the rustle of bank-notes.'

It is Kouli now who suffers from the blazing darts of the sun.

'Kouli we'll go to Sine's. Then, after the midday prayer we can drive around again.'

Mour thinks of the beggars now without any ill-feeling. 'All in all, they don't deserve our scorn … In any case, we only despise them when we don't need them … We shall have to find some way of letting them get back their rights as citizens … create some organisations to which they can be assimilated … carry out a vast campaign of rehabilitation on their behalf … They need to be educated, as do a large part of the population … No, they aren't the only ones who are left out …'

The house which Mour has bought for Sine is a luxurious villa situated on the Corniche; throughout the day the air is fresh with cool sea-breezes. The creaking of the heavy iron gate awakens Mour from the drowsy state into which he had lapsed while thinking of a society in which begging would be neither the expression of want, nor the manifestation of a form of greed. He had seen in a city in the north of the country, the extraordinary case of a beggar who attracted the respect and admiration of the whole population. This man only begged once a week, on the night of Thursday to Friday. This was for him the occasion to pay tribute to God's might and sing the praises of the glory of the Prophet. When the people who had waited for a whole week for this moment and had already prepared their offerings heard his voice which penetrated deep into their hearts and cast its spell over them, they rushed zealously to their doors, where he waited only a few moments; they offered him money, rice or millet and they had the chance to admire the immense height of the old man, dressed majestically in an ample white or indigo boubou stiff with starch, worn over an equally ample *turki*, from which a kind of small tab, at the neck, pressed against the Adam's apple of the venerable blind old gentleman, leaning on his stick.

Mour found Sine in the dining-room, sitting at the table waiting for her coffee, a cigarette in her mouth. The fury with which he shouted at Sine was the expression of his own bitterness and resentment.

'Sine, I've told you I don't like to see you smoking. I have formally forbidden you to smoke, and I thought that that had been understood!'

By way of reply, Sine simply drew deeply on her cigarette and blew a long wisp of smoke towards the ceiling.

'Sine, it's you I'm talking to! Will you please put out that cigarette!'

As Mour thunders at her, he simultaneously walks over to her and sends the cigarette flying, as well as the cup of coffee that a servant has just placed on the table. The white curtains and Mour's boubou are splashed. Sine gets up to avoid staining her dress. She stares at Mour insolently, and shouts back, 'If you think I'm prepared to be stuck here like a piece of furniture and receive your orders and your prohibitions, then you're making a mistake! I'm a person and not a block of wood!'

'You're taking leave of your senses, Sine! You don't know what you're saying ...'

'You're the one who's raving mad! What are you thinking about? That I'm here just to satisfy your whims? – No! I'm your wife, so treat me like a wife. Really, Mour, if you think I'm going to let you treat me like a common-or-garden object, then you've got another think coming! Monsieur disappears for days on end and when he reappears it's to start giving me orders! Oh, no, Mour! You can do that to your Lolli, but I'm no sheep!'

'Lolli is a very worthy, respectable woman! I think that if you'd looked at yourself in a mirror, with a cigarette dangling out of your mouth, you'd see how you belittle yourself! Your hair cut so short, you look as if you'd shaved it and all that lipstick, all that causes me very deep displeasure!'

'We don't talk the same language! ... We shall never talk the same language.'

'Not as long as you ape habits and ways of behaving that don't suit you!'

'No; because you argue like someone out of the Middle Ages. And besides, if you stop to think, that's how you found me when you married me. Now you want me to change simply because I've become your wife. It's not logical! You ought to be able to put up with me just as you found me.'

Mour is heavy-hearted. It's true that it was not till several months after his marriage to Sine that he realised that certain things upset him, shocked him even, but he had always hoped that he would be able to make his wife see reason, for he had thought he had managed to make her give up smoking, using lipstick and wearing tight trousers.

'If today she's starting doing things again that she knows I hate the most, it's undoubtedly out of a wish to provoke me ... I fell into the trap ... I ought not to have ...'

Mour waited a long time for a lunch which no one served. With an empty stomach and a heavy head, he had to resign himself to praying and setting off again in the van, seated next to Kouli.

A torrid heat blazes down in this early afternoon. Mour feels as if burning coals are at his temples. He asks Kouli to begin at the Main Market. Then they go the rounds of the three hospitals in the City; then they visit each one of the countless mosques; they go to every one of the squares and all the beggars' vantage points, but the beggars have not turned up as agreed. On Salla Niang's instructions, they are continuing their strike.

After Mour's last visit some of them, moved by the supplications of someone who didn't give the impression of being a bad man, and anxious to respect the pact that they had made together – he by giving his money, and they by giving their word – had decided to go to take up their positions in the streets. With her last energy, Salla Niang harangued them.

'What! It's out of the question; it's completely out of the question! Just because he threw his money at us, we have to give in to his whims! No! If he threw his money about, it's because he'd got his pockets full, it's because he can afford to throw it about by the handful. What we managed to pick up – *sunu wersek la*! – is just our good luck! If you go out on the streets you'll seem like miserable weak-kneed creatures, with no dignity, who can't be relied on … Remember what decided you to hole up here! No! Nobody budges from here!'

The van drives round and round and round. Kouli, realising his employer's anger and distress, does not dare ask him what they should do next. He keeps on driving about in the van, wondering from time to time if Mour realises that they have driven round the City more than ten times: Main Market, hospitals, mosques, the main squares, in front of the big shops, and even the most obscure corners of the City. Not a sign of a beggar, not a sign of a *bàttu*. The sun starts to set, sets lower and lower … It is the first hour of twilight.

'Kouli, go back to their house. We must go and give them this meat.'

'I beg your pardon, sir?'

'I said you must drive to the beggars' house. We can't keep this meat all night in this heat. We must go and give it to them.'

'Right, sir.'

'Then you can take me back to Sine's house. Tomorrow you must come and pick me up at half past four in the morning, to drive me to the village where you took the little man – the little Serigne – with the blue boubou and the huge chéchia.'

'Yes, sir … Perhaps I'd better go and warn my family and then come and spend the night at your house to be ready to start early.'

Mour scarcely heard what Kouli said. His thoughts were already drifting between the way the beggars had cheated him, the impudence – no, the barefaced brazenness – of 'that woman who undoutedly manipulates them', the insolence of the 'jackanapes of a blind beggar' and the sheer madness of Keba Dabo.

'All my troubles arise from having chosen Keba Dabo as my assistant ... For this type of delicate operation I ought to have chosen someone more mature, who would have found a solution to the problem by negotiation ... Keba is a hot-head ... One day he'll come a cropper.'

When Kouli opened the door of the van for him to alight, Mour dragged himself towards the sitting-room. Completely fagged-out, he dropped into an armchair, not even having the strength to go up to his room and change.

He didn't harbour any resentment against Sine. After the quarrel, just as he was getting into the van, after the midday prayer, he had thought to himself that he shouldn't have stayed away the whole time it was her 'turn'. 'After all, it must be upsetting for a woman ...' He reproached himself also for not having given her any explanation. He came to the conclusion that their misunderstandings arose from the great difference in age between them, and because of this it was his duty, as the older, to make certain concessions, insofar as they were not prejudicial to his authority nor in any way detrimental to his respectability.

'Dinner is ready, sir.'

Mour raised his head slightly, without answering the cook. He is exhausted. How long is it since he had a good night's sleep? How long is it since he ate his fill as he liked to, with tastily prepared dishes? – He has not counted the days since everything has ceased to have any meaning for him, except his appointment as Vice-President of the Republic, the image of the mysterious and henceforth elusive Kifi Bokoul, and the beggars' resistance. Even Serigne Birama has slipped out of his universe. The beggars, Kifi Bokoul, the Vice-Presidency ... The beggars, Kifi Bokoul, the Vice-Presidency ...

Mour is dog-tired. Physically and mentally. To be made a fool of by the beggars, what an irony of fate! His whole

body aches, especially his lower back and his shoulders …
'It must be the huge quarters of meat I lifted this morning
… I shall have to start doing exercises again.'

No, he won't eat; he'll just have a glass of hot milk
before going to bed; or better still an infusion of *kinkiliba*
and a glass of hot milk.

He sees Sine sit down at table. Sine has not spoken a
word to him; she doesn't know that he has forgotten their
quarrel at midday. He even tries to concentrate all his
attention till Sine has finished her dinner to see if she is
going to smoke again. He must have fallen asleep again as
he only comes to when the signature tune announcing the
television news catches his ear. He opens his eyes and sees
Sine sit down on the couch, after switching on the
television. He remembers that he has to look and see if she
has been smoking, but just as he turns his eyes towards
Sine, the news reader's voice announces, in the solemn
tone that gives him the impression that he is speaking face
to face with God:

'Whereas the Constitution;

– Whereas the decree of the 6th of June, bearing on the
revision of the Constitution; etc.,

The President of the Republic decrees that

Firstly, Monsieur Toumane Sane's functions as Home
Secretary shall be terminated.

Secondly, Monsieur Toumane Sane is hereby appointed
Vice-President of the Republic …'

Also in Longman African Classics

Fools and other stories

Njabulo Ndebele

Winner of the Noma Award 1983

'And when victims spit upon victims should they not be called fools? Fools of darkness.'

A taut, lyrical and compelling collection of stories, vividly bringing to life the black urban locations of apartheid South Africa.

These are rich and enchanting stories told with the warmth of childhood memory: of the adulation of a child for his trumpet-playing uncle; a teenager's trial of endurance to prove himself worthy of his street-gang; a child's rebellion against his parents snobbish aspirations.

And the title story, *Fools,* tells with painful intensity of events sparked by a meeting between a disgraced teacher, haunted by the impotence of his present life, and a student activist railing against those who do not share his sense of urgency.

The author believes 'we have given away too much of our real and imaginative lives to the oppressor'. These beautiful award-winning stories of township life in all its complexity are his answer.

'Njabulo Ndebele's first book represents the kind of beginning in fiction that will prove to have altered the contours of our literature ... His storytelling is full-fleshed and elegant ... of thrilling significance'.

Lionel Abrahams *Sesame*

'Brings with it an exhilarating current of fresh air ... solid, vibrant prose'.

E'skia Mphahlele *The Sowetan*

ISBN 0 582 78621 5

Hungry Flames and other Black South African Short Stories

Edited by Mbulelo Mzamane

From the bare concrete of the crowded prisons to the carpeted drawing rooms of the new African middle class, these fifteen short stories by South Africa's finest Black writers paint an urgent and vital picture of contemporary South Africa.

These stories rank with those of Steinbeck and Hemingway in their honest portraits of working men and women in all their strengths and in all their weaknesses — all of them living in the shadow of the apartheid state.

Over fifty years of Black South African writing in English is represented in this collection. A critical introduction describes the evolution of writing from the pioneers, such as R.R.R. Dhlomo and Sol Plaatje, through the urban 'jazz' style of the fifties to the more politicised Black Consciousness writers of the Sharpeville and Soweto eras.

The editor, Mbulelo Mzamane, is himself a distinguished writer of short stories and is the author of *My Cousin Comes to Jo'burg* (1982) and of *The Children of Soweto* (1982). He now teaches in the Department of English, Ahmadu Bello University, Zaria in Nigeria.

ISBN 0 582 78590 1

The Last Duty

Isidore Okpewho

Winner of the African Arts Prize for Literature

Against the backcloth of a violent and murderous civil war six individuals linked by conflicting ties of honour, greed, lust, fear and love play out a drama of their own that is no less bloody than the war itself. The resolution of the drama has the cathartic force of classical tragedy as the individuals recognise their final duty to reclaim their self-respect from the quagmire of corruption and betrayal into which they have all been led.

'The Last Duty is a highly sophisticated and successfully achieved piece of work ... an imaginative reconstruction of the experience of the Nigerian Civil War. In its deep moral concern and in its technical accomplishment, The Last Duty has earned an honourable place in the development of African literature'.

British Book News

'C'est un beau livre' *Afrique Contemporaine*

'A strong and original voice in Nigerian literature'
Books Abroad

ISBN 0 582 78535 9

Scarlet Song

Mariama Ba

Translated by Dorothy S. Blair

Mariama Ba's first novel So Long a Letter was the winner of the Noma Award in 1980. In this her second and, tragically, last novel she displays all the same virtues of warmth and crusading zeal for women's rights that won her so many admirers for her earlier work.

Mireille, daughter of a French diplomat and Ousmane, son of a poor Muslim family in Senegal, are two childhood sweethearts forced to share their love in secret. Their marriage shocks and dismays both sets of parents, but it soon becomes clear that their youthful optimism and love offer a poor defence against the pressures of society. As Ousmane is lured back to his roots, Mireille is left humiliated, isolated and alone.

The tyranny of tradition and chauvinism is brilliantly exposed in this passionate plea for human understanding. The author's sympathetic insights into the condition of women deserve recognition throughout the world.

ISBN 0 582 78595 2

Tales of Amadou Koumba

Birago Diop

Translated by Dorothy S. Blair

Retold with wit and charm, this classic collection of folk tales by the 'poet of the African bush' stands comparison with the fables of Aesop and La Fontaine. Originally told to Diop by his family's *griot,* these tales take us back and forth between the surreal world of the miraculous and the profound reality of African daily life.

'The poetic nature of Birago Diop's writing, in its primitive majesty, is in direct line from the Griots and the oral tradition'.

Jean-Paul Sartre

'Everything in this subtle and perceptive work is a delight'. *Présence Africaine*

'This show of African wisdom, constitutes, without a shadow of doubt, the finest prose work in our African literature'.

Afrique en Marche

ISBN 0 582 78587 1